The Rules of
Project Risk Management

This is a well-researched and authoritative book on managing risks in projects. It is written by an acknowledged expert who has devoted his lifetime career to the study and application of risk management. Its approach is aligned with the international standard, "Risk Management Principles and Guidelines", ISO 31000, and it presents key principles for managing project risks. However, the unique feature is its structure, based on 22 practical guidelines, called "rules". The author suggests that, as an alternative to reading the book cover to cover, the reader might prefer to peruse individual rules when time permits. Anyone involved in project or risk management should read this book.

Mike Nichols, Founder and Chairman of The Nichols Group,
Chairman of the Association for Project Management and
Board Member of the Major Projects Association

Rob Chapman's book is highly unusual but completely invaluable in taking a case study based approach to a subject that often is confused by an excess of jargon and process. Dr Chapman draws on an extensive international range of real projects to demonstrate how things can so easily go wrong, and what project managers can learn from high profile failures. I thoroughly recommend this book to anyone involved in project and programme management.

Steve Fowler, CEO, The Institute of Risk Management, UK

A unique combination of the foundations of project management and the latest trend in risk management standardisation with clear alignment with the ISO 31000 risk management standard.

Alex Dali, President,
The Global Institute for Risk Management Standards, France

More than ever, larger, more complex and more expensive projects are required in a severely constrained global economy. The Rules of Project Risk Management *is essential reading, not merely for the project management professional but for all stakeholders who have a keen interest in leveraging better results from project investments. Whether a project is executed for commercial or social benefit, the insights given in this book are invaluable. Chapman shares his vast experience in risk management through practical case studies and pertinent guidance tools. He deals with the factors which have habitually influenced performance but refreshingly provides beneficial insight into the delicate factors of human psyche and behaviour which have been little understood or quantified for the influence they bear in managing project risk. Proactive and sustained risk management is rightly placed at the heart of project success.*

Moira Moses, Group Executive,
Transnet Capital Projects (2007–2012), South Africa

Dr. Chapman's book is extremely timely. All projects are subject to risk, the challenge is to identify and effectively manage risk. Project risk management is a rapidly emerging tool, but is often not well understood by executive and senior management. Dr. Chapman's book is a must read for anyone responsible for profit and loss as well as project delivery. The book is structured in a concise effective manner with outstanding case studies that bring life to the concepts and theory through real life examples of success and failure. This is a book that I will keep close by for ready reference.

Thomas Topolski, Senior Vice President and
Managing Director, Middle East North Africa, Louis Berger, Qatar

I had the pleasure and privilege of working with Dr Chapman on the Transnet Capital expansion Program in South Africa, one of the largest centrally-managed programs of projects the country has seen. In his capacity as Program Practice Lead for Risk Management, Dr Chapman brought a level of expertise and experience and instituted processes that served us proud. The Program was a major success, and Dr Chapman's oversight of Risk Management at multiple levels was a significant contributor to that. I am delighted that he has authored this book which I know will help us all deliver projects more successfully.

Alan Grey, Managing Director-Industrial Infrastructure,
Global Director-Gateway Logistics, Hatch Goba, South Africa

The Rules of Project Risk Management

Implementation Guidelines for Major Projects

Robert J. Chapman

GOWER

Published by
Gower Publishing Limited
Wey Court East
Union Road
Farnham
Surrey, GU9 7PT
England

Ashgate Publishing Company
110 Cherry Street
Suite 3-1
Burlington, VT 05401-3818
USA

www.gowerpublishing.com

British Library Cataloguing in Publication Data
A catalogue record for this book is available from the British Library.

Library of Congress Cataloging-in-Publication Data
Chapman, Robert J.
 The rules of project risk management : implementation guidelines for major projects / by Robert James Chapman.
    pages cm
 Includes bibliographical references and index.
  ISBN 978-1-4724-1195-2 (hardback) -- ISBN 978-1-4724-1196-9 (ebook) -- ISBN 978-1-4724-1197-6 (epub) 1. Risk management. 2. Project management. I. Title.
  HD61.C4937 2013
  658.4'04--dc23
                                                                    2013025796
 ISBN 9781472411952 (hbk)
 ISBN 9781472411969 (ebk – PDF)
 ISBN 9781472411976 (ebk – ePUB)

Printed in the United Kingdom by Henry Ling Limited, at the Dorset Press, Dorchester, DT1 1HD

This book is dedicated to Sir Ranulph Fiennes, a veteran of successful project risk management. He is described by the *Guinness Book of Records* as "The World's Greatest Living Explorer". His remarkable and world-renowned accomplishments include the following:

- First to reach both Poles.
- First to cross the Antarctic and the Arctic Ocean.
- First to circumnavigate the world along its polar axis. This three-year, 52,000-mile odyssey took intricate planning, 1,900 sponsors, a 52-person team to handle, complex communications, meticulous planning and an iron determination mixed with flexibility. The circumnavigation has never been successfully repeated.
- Winner of ITV Greatest Britons 2007 Sport Award.
- 1968/1969: led the first hovercraft expedition up the longest river in the world (the Nile).
- 1990: achieved the world record for unsupported northerly polar travel.
- 1992: led the team that discovered the lost city of Ubar on the Yemeni border (after seven previous search expeditions over a 26-year period).
- 1992/1993: achieved a world first by completing the first unsupported crossing of the Antarctic continent. This was the longest unsupported polar journey in history.
- 2003: achieved the first 7x7x7 (seven marathons in seven consecutive days on all seven continents).
- 2005: climbed Everest (Tibet side) to within 300 m of summit.
- 2007: climbed the North Face of the Eiger.
- 2008: climbed Everest (Nepal side) to within 400 m of the summit.
- 2009: successfully summited Everest with Thundu Sherpa.

Contents

List of Figures

List of Tables

List of Case Studies

About the Author

Dr Robert Chapman, FIRM, FAPM, FICM, PMI-RMP, is currently the Head of Risk Management for the MMC and Gamuda Joint Venture which is fulfilling the role of Project Delivery Partner for the Klang Valley Mass Rapid Transit Project in Malaysia. Prior to this appointment, he was a Director of Risk Management at AECOM, Hornagold & Hills, Capro Consulting and Osprey Project Management and the Programme Lead for risk management on the HMG joint venture in South Africa, supporting the Parastatal Transnet. He has provided risk management services in England, the Netherlands, Ireland, South Africa, Qatar, UAE and Malaysia to companies within the rail, pharmaceutical, aviation, marine, broadcast, heritage, water, health, sport, oil and gas, property development, construction and transportation industries, as well to local authorities in the public sector. He has had articles published by *Enterprise Risk* (South Africa), *ExtraProtect* (translated into French and German), *IT Adviser*, *Yorkshire Post*, *Strategic Risk*, *PLC Strategies*, *Project*, the *Architects' Journal* and *PropertyWeek* and has refereed papers published by the *Journal of International Project Management* and *Construction Management & Economics*. He was made a Fellow of the Institute of Risk Management (UK), the Association for Project Management (UK) and the Institute of Commercial Management (UK) for his contribution to the development of the discipline of risk management. He has been recognised by both Transnet in South Africa and the Association for Project Management in the UK as having exceptional risk management skills. He was awarded a PhD in risk management from the University of Reading in 1998 for research into the impact of changes in personnel on the delivery of investment projects. In addition, he has completed research on the subject of risk management on behalf of the Architects Registration Council of the United Kingdom (ARCUK). His book *Retaining Design Team Members: A Risk Management Approach* was published by RIBA Enterprises in 2002 and examines the causes behind employee turnover, the impact it can have and the risk mitigation actions that can be implemented to reduce the likelihood of occurrence. His *second book Simple Tools and Techniques for Enterprise Risk Management* was first published in

2006 and the second edition was published in 2011. It is on sale in 40 countries around the world and is recommended reading in universities in the USA, the UK, Malaysia, Malta, India, Singapore and Australia. The second edition is a prescribed book for the UNISA (South Africa) postgraduate degree entitled "Enterprise Risk Management". He was a contributory author of the Office of Government Commerce's 2007 publication *Management of Risk: Guidance for Practitioners*, which supports the Prince2 Project Management methodology. Subsequent to passing the Management of Risk Practitioner exam, he became an accredited M_o_R (Management of Risk) trainer, providing risk management training to a number of diverse companies. He was part of the reference group which was consulted prior to the preparation of the OGC portfolio, programme and project management maturity model (P3M3®). Prior to its publication, he reviewed and commented upon risk management International Standard ISO 31000 on behalf of the British Standards Institution. In November 2013 he was shortlisted (in the category "Managing Risk Across Boundaries") for the IRM Global Risk Awards 2014. In addition, he has provided IT risk management guidance to the Chartered Institute of Accountants England and Wales in the form of a risk management handbook.

Foreword

Robert J. Chapman's book, *The Rules of Project Risk Management: Implementation Guidelines for Major Projects* is a thoughtful, engaging and illustrative work that board members and senior managers in particular will find most instructive and unique. It combines an innovative synthesis of the foundations of project management and the latest trend in risk management standardisation, with clear alignment with the ISO 31000 risk management standard. As the concept of uncertainty is definitively linked to the achievements of a project's objectives, readers will discover the vocabulary, the principles, the framework and the risk management process proposed in the ISO 31000 standard in a practical and pragmatic way. Certainly, managers will be familiar with examples and case studies in project management, but this book will guide the reader to structure and take risk-balanced decisions in an uncertain environment in order to achieve his or her objectives. Before you set about trying to design or change your project, read this book first.

Alex Dali,
President, Global Institute for Risk Management Standards

Preface

The nuclear, space exploration, aeronautical, oil and gas, pharmaceutical, road, media, rail, water, energy, information technology, finance, mining, defence and construction sectors (among others) are now embracing risk management. Major infrastructure projects around the world commonly have a designated risk manager or managers (or personnel with the same function but a different label). More and more industries are adopting risk management. There is a growing academic base for the subject. The risk management function has been transformed in recent years and for listed businesses is now firmly entrenched as a board-level concern.

While there is a plethora of books, papers and articles on the subject of project risk management, they commonly (but not exclusively) focus on the theory and process of risk management. This book attempts to provide a more practical approach, albeit still with reference to some of the underlying principles. To satisfy this goal, this book describes a set of implementation guidelines for project risk management to aid inculcating risk with a project's culture. The guidelines are aimed at providing practical experience-based guidance for effective risk management. While they are written in the manner of a series of "rules" to provide clear direction, they should not be regarded as hard and fast, mandatory activities. The reason for this is that project risk management must be tailored to suit a project's context and circumstances. The "rules" are not arranged in any particular order of importance – the first ones are not more important than later ones and vice versa. Read them all and then start to put them into practice, adopting those that seem most relevant to the current stage of your project. A lot of them will flow together so that if appropriate, you can carry them out simultaneously. In addition, a number of what I have termed "mini" case studies have been included to provide real-world examples of success and failure in project delivery and a reason (or reasons) behind the outcome which offers a rich insight into project performance. They have been kept short to strive to ensure that they did not swamp the book or lose their focus. Without exaggeration, they were fascinating to research and read about.

Before we begin, because the anticipated audience for this book is broad, it is worth pausing to answer the following questions: what is risk? What is project risk? What is project risk management? And what is the role of risk managers?

Definition of risk: concern over risk relates to the ability to achieve objectives. Risk is defined within the broad based International Standard ISO 31000 (entitled "Risk Management – Principles and Guidelines") as "effect of uncertainty on objectives". A further definition, again focusing on the realisation of objectives, is provided by the *Management of Risk: Guidance for Practitioners* (2010 edition) guide, published on behalf of the Office of Government Commerce, which states risk is "an uncertain event (or set of events) that should it occur will have an effect on objectives". The UK Association for Project Management (APM)[1] definition is very similar and describes risk as "an uncertain event or set of circumstances that should it occur or they occur will have an effect on achievement of one or more project objectives". Other definitions go on to draw attention to the fact that a risk may be negative or positive. These two types of project risk are called threat and opportunity respectively. It is rarely advisable to focus on reducing threats without giving consideration to exploiting associated opportunities, just as it is inadvisable to pursue opportunities without giving careful measured consideration to the associated threats. A corollary of businesses-pursuing opportunities through executing projects is exposure to threats. Given the need to recognise both types of risk and their dimensions, an earlier definition of risk is helpful. The US Project Management Institute (PMI) describes risk as "an uncertain event or condition that, if it occurs, has a positive or negative effect on a project's objectives".[2]

Definition of project risk: a definition of project risk is found in British Standard BS 31100 (2008): "risk relating to delivery of a product or service, usually with the constraints of time, cost and quality". A possible definition of project risk which takes account of the downside (negative) and upside (positive) nature of risk is as follows: project risk is the likelihood of a negative or positive event impacting on a project's declared objectives.

---

1   APM (2006) *APM Body of Knowledge*, 5th edn. Princes Risborough: APM Publishing Ltd.
2   PMI (2009) *A Guide to the Project Management Body of Knowledge (PMBOK® Guide)*, 4th edn. Newtown Square, Pennsylvania: Project Management Institute. An American National Standard, ANSI/PMI 99-001-2008. The same definition is provided for "project risk" and is included in PMI (2009), *Practice Standard for Project Risk Management*. Newtown Square, Pennsylvania: Project Management Institute.

Definition of project risk management: ISO 31000 defines "risk" as "effect of uncertainty on objectives" whereas "project risk management" (PRM) refers to the management of that exposure in the pursuit of achieving predefined goals. Hence, PRM has two primary functions: a management activity (the "what") to drive down the exposure to threats and exploit opportunities, and a goal-seeking function to support the satisfaction of a project's aims or objectives (the "why"). Consequently, PRM requires both a support management process and comprehension of the project's objectives. (Typically, objectives include cost, time and quality; however, they may also include goals relating to cost-in-use, the environment, maintainability, reliability, reputation, safety, scope and sustainability.) There are a number of descriptions and definitions of PRM, but they only focus on one facet, the "what", and not the "why". Examples are included in the bulletpoints below:

- Patel and Morris[3] describe PRM as a process, but omit reference to the fact that its overarching goal is to secure the achievement of a project's objectives: "The process of identification, assessment, allocation, and management of all project risks."

- The fourth edition of the PMI's *PMBOK® Guide* states that: "The objectives of Project Risk Management are to increase the probability and impact of positive events and decrease the probability and impact of negative events in the project."

- ISO 31000:2009 defines risk management as the "coordinated activities to direct and control an organization with regard to risk".

Reflecting on the primary aim of PRM, a possible definition is as follows: PRM is a proactive management process designed to exploit opportunities and treat threats to secure a project's agreed, defined and disseminated objectives.

Definition of consequence: outcome of an event affecting objectives (ISO 31000:2009).

Definition of event: an occurrence or change of a particular set of circumstances (ISO 31000:2009).

---

3   Patel, M.B. and Morris, P.W.G. (1999) *Guide to the Project Management Body of Knowledge*. Manchester: Centre for Research in the Management of Projects (CRMP), University of Manchester.

Definition of novel technology: a novel or new technology is one which is either still under development and has no history of proven performance or has a very short history of proven performance. A novel technology may be also described as one which has not been tested or evaluated to the same degree as proven technologies and or has not received regulatory approval.

Definition of opportunity: a positive risk, an uncertain event that could have a favourable impact on a project's objectives or benefits (see other definitions in the *APM Body of Knowledge* and the M_o_R Guide).

Definition of threat: a negative risk, an uncertain event that could have a negative impact on a project's objectives or benefits (see other definitions in the *APM Body of Knowledge* and the M_o_R Guide).

Definition of risk mitigation: a risk treatment that deals with a negative consequence (ISO Guide 73:2009). The word "mitigate" is described in the *Oxford Everyday Dictionary* (1981) as "to make less intense or serious or severe". Risk mitigation refers to reducing a threat but not removing it in its entirety.

Role of a project risk manager: in essence, the role of the risk manager (or a similarly named position) is to assist in defining and supporting the delivery of a project's risk management objectives. The role description needs to be tailored to the organisation's objectives, risk management maturity, frameworks, policies, plans, procedures, reporting requirements, audit processes and stakeholder (and/or contractual) commitments. Typical duties involve preparing, reviewing and or approving the risk management framework, policy, plan and procedures, facilitating risk workshops and meetings, contributing to the preparation of the business case and feasibility studies, supporting the selection of the procurement route and the form of contract, carrying out quantitative risk analysis as required, overseeing the implementation of risk management in the supply chain and risk reporting. Each organisation, programme or project must make it abundantly apparent to its project personnel that risk management is everyone's responsibility in the same way as the delivery of quality and safety are.

Acknowledgements

In writing this book, I owe a debt of gratitude to work colleagues past and present. First of all, I acknowledge and thank former colleague Tarek Mourad (Chief Engineer, Civil Infrastructure at AECOM Middle East) for his observations and suggestions on the text generally (based on his knowledge of the implementation of major infrastructure projects), but particularly on the "Structure of the book" section, to improve the reader's ability to navigate the book. I thank my colleague Mohd Zairi Poniran for his comments and observations. I record my appreciation of the review conducted by Graham Williams of GSW Consultancy Limited and thank him for his thought-provoking comments (Graham is a consultant, trainer, assessor and author specialising in programme, project and risk management and a former Chief Examiner of the M_o_R course – based on *Management of Risk: Guidance for Practitioners* published by the Office of Government Commerce. He was a co-author of the 2007 edition of the publication and mentor to the author of the 2010 edition). My thanks also go to Alex Dali (President of the Global Institute for Risk Management Standards) for his detailed comments in relation to International Standard ISO 31000, his support and encouragement for this book in general and the preparation of the foreword. I wish to spotlight the continued support received from Steve Fowler of the Institute of Risk Management following his endorsement of this and my last book, the second edition of *Simple Tools and Techniques for Enterprise Risk Management* published in 2011 by John Wiley & Sons. I thank the Global Institute for Risk Management Standards and the Institute of Risk Management for supporting this book and recommending it to their members. I thank the MRT Corporation of Malaysia for its kind approval to publish Case Study 26, which describes the Klang Valley Mass Rapid Transit Project (which forms part of the Greater Kuala Lumpur/Klang Valley (GKL/KV) National Key Economic Area (NKEA)). I thank the National Audit Office for its kind permission to include extracts from or make reference to project audits that it has published. At the request of the National Audit Office, I advise that "use within this text of National

Audit Office (NAO) material does not indicate any endorsement by the NAO of this publication, or the material contained within it". I thank Audit Scotland for its kind permission to include extracts of the 2004 Auditor General's report entitled "Management of the Holyrood Building Project" licensed under the Open Government Licence. I record the kind approval afforded by Steven Cross, RIBA Enterprises Director of Partnerships, to reproduce the illustration of alternative procurement methods included in Figure 3.4. I thank Rob Mathie, Assistant Auditor-General, Performance Audit of the New South Wales government, Australia for granting permission to include extracts of the audit report describing the Millennium Train Project. Inclusion of the *Gateway Lessons Learned Key Themes 2010/2011* published by the UK Department of Finance and Personnel (http://www.dfpni.gov.uk) was sanctioned under the Open Government Licence. The information has not been changed in any way. I acknowledge and thank David Hillson for permission to include an extract of his paper "Towards a Risk Maturity Model" published in the *International Journal of Project and Business Risk Management* (1)1 in 1997. (The Risk Maturity Model is described in more detail in David's informative book entitled *Effective Opportunity Management for Projects: Exploiting Positive Risk*, published in 2004 by Taylor & Francis.) I thank the Institute of Commercial Management for permission to use their logo and offering to recommend the book to its members. Last but not least, my thanks go to the endorsers of the book, the majority of whom I have worked with at some time in the past.

Audience

This book is written for a diverse range of audiences, but specifically new project risk practitioners wishing to extend their skills, competent risk practitioners who may be looking to broaden their approach and those engaged in risk training. It is also written for lecturers and graduate and undergraduate students, members of the Institute of Risk Management,[1] members of the Global Institute for Risk Management Standard G31000,[2] members of the Association for Project Management, members of the Project Management Institute (USA), , members of the Institute of Commercial Management, change agents, portfolio managers, programme managers, project managers, government department risk leads and consultant and construction companies developing their internal project risk management discipline.

---

1   The Institute of Risk Management (IRM) describes itself as "the world's leading enterprise-wide risk education Institute". Following the publication of ISO 31000, the IRM, in conjunction with AIRMIC (Association of Insurance and Risk Managers in Industry and Commerce (UK)) and Alarm, published a short document entitled "A Structured Approach to Enterprise Risk Management (ERM) and the Requirements of ISO 31000".

2   The Global Institute for Risk Management Standards has created a platform called G31000 which supports the development and raises the awareness of ISO 31000:2009, an International Standard for Risk Management (which was published on 13 November 2009) together with the accompanying standard, ISO/IEC 31010:2009 – Risk Assessment Techniques and the Risk Management vocabulary ISO Guide 73 (updated in 2009 with revised terms and definitions).

How to Read this Book

Time is precious. Projects typically have a specific end-date objective which forces a pace in terms of completing the life cycle stages. The time between interim deadlines can be particularly short. As a consequence, commonly there is very limited opportunity for quiet reflection. In particular, how much time do we ever have in any one day to reflect on what we are doing, how we are doing it and whether there is a better approach? Hence, this book is purposefully written in such a way that it is hoped that readers can quickly find and focus on the subjects that interest them rather than having to carry out an extensive search for the instructive guidance they seek. The appropriate approach to reading this book will depend on your exposure and experience of risk management and where your specific interests lie. The intention is that dividing the book into a number of short simple rules means that a rule can be easily read on the train to work, during a coffee break, prior to a meeting or waiting for a flight. Time does not need to be set aside to read this book. It can be read during those intervals in the day that are sometimes forced upon us.

1

Structure of the Book

While the structure of the book has its genesis in the International Standard ISO 31000:2009, "Risk Management – Principles and Guidelines"[1,2] (subsequently referred to as ISO 31000 or simply the Standard), it is also influenced by the EFQM Excellence Model (see Appendix A), together with systems and system dynamics (see Appendix B) and the common causes of project failure described by the Department of Finance and Personnel, Northern Ireland (DFPNI) and the UK Cabinet Office' (see Appendix C). The selection of the Standard as a suitable structure is based on its declared scope, applicability, popularity and geographical reach. The declared scope of the Standard is to provide *principles and generic guidelines* on the implementation of risk management. In other words, it is not a rigid rule-based document. It states that it can be applied to any public, private or community enterprise (and association, group or individual), throughout the life of an organisation and to a wide range of projects. Since its publication in 2009, it architects and advocates have declared that it has enjoyed international popularity and adoption. Part of this popularity may stem from the fact that it builds on numerous earlier risk management publications and does not markedly deviate from risk management practices of the last 20 years.[3] It is promoted

---

1   Commentators have observed that ISO 31000 describes itself as a "generic approach" and a "guideline" as well as an "International Standard". A standard typically means a written definition, limit or rule approved and monitored for compliance by an authoritative agency (or professional or recognised body) as a minimum acceptable benchmark. A guideline is recommended practice that allows some discretion or leeway in its interpretation, implementation or use. Clearly, a standard and a guideline have very different purposes. It is considered that the adoption of this guideline is appropriate for a book which examines the practicalities of the implementation of project risk management (PRM).

2   The Standard is published by the International Organization for Standardization, commonly known by the acronym "ISO". Since its inception in 1947, the ISO has published more than 19,000 international standards covering almost all aspects of technology and business. ISO defines a standard as a document that provides requirements, specifications, guidelines or characteristics that can be used consistently to ensure that materials, products, processes and services are fit for purpose.

3   See, for instance, CCTA (1993) "Introduction to the Management of Risk", produced by the Government Centre for Information Systems and published on behalf of HMSO.

by the Global Institute for Risk Management Standards and at the time of writing the LinkedIn group dedicated to ISO 31000 has over 23,000 members. The geographical reach of the Standard is evident by the fact that it has been adopted by 41 countries as their national risk management standard and has been translated into 22 languages. Given its general appeal (whilst recognising that it is not without its critics), it appeared appropriate to adopt the Standard to structure a book describing the practicalities of implementing PRM.

Structure of the Standard

Included within the Standard is the following figure (see Figure 1.1 below), which it states illustrates the relationship between the principles, the framework and the process. These are the three main elements of the Standard. All other aspects of the Standard are described within these three elements.

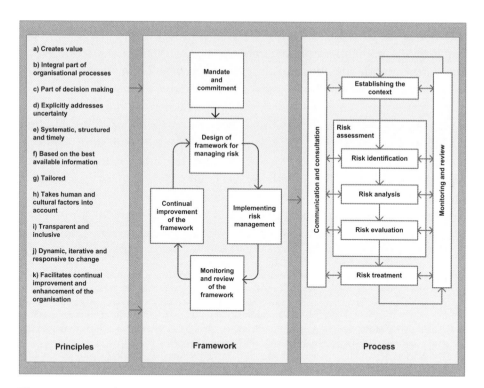

Figure 1.1   **Relationship between the risk management principles, framework and process**

However, it could be argued that this figure does not help the reader as much as it might to assimilate the valuable content of the Standard and that the principles or framework are not a natural starting point. The Standard itself implies a different sequence from the one illustrated in Figure 1.1.

There should be a discussion of the context, stakeholders and existing risk management competencies prior to a discussion of the framework. In addition, with regard to the context, there should be reference to how a project relates to its organisation and how that organisation relates to its environment. Observations on the Standard are included in Appendix D.

A Model or Interpretation of ISO 31000 for Projects

A model of ISO 31000 is proposed here (see Figure 1.2 below) which stems from a systems view of the world that illustrates one aspect of the Standard being a subset of another. An organisation (Organisation A) sits within an external environment and within that organisation is the leadership function which controls the project stakeholders, the resources and the systems (a group term adopted for the risk framework, policy, plan and individual procedures). This way of looking at risk management is based on concepts described in an article[4] and a refereed paper[5] that I have written. The model included here illustrates that multiple organisations sit within the environment, where some external organisations impact on Organisation A (inward arrow), are affected by Organisation A (outward arrow) and engage in contracts with Organisation A (bi-directional arrows). In addition, others that are not affected by, engage with or impact Organisation A are labelled "Independent Organisations". The reason for the inclusion of these other organisations is that as projects grow in scale and complexity, the greater their dependency will be (in terms of a project realising its objectives) on third parties. While not all projects are construction projects, consider for example the number of organisations that will have been involved in constructing Terminal 5 at London Heathrow Airport, the buildings erected for the 2012 London Olympics and the Burj Khalifa tower in Dubai. Furthermore, consider for instance the number of suppliers that are involved in the manufacturing process of a plane, ship or train. The model is composed of layered concentric squares with the most significant on the upper level and the

---

4   Chapman, R.J. (1995) "No Need to Gamble on Risks", *The Architect's Journal*, 30 November, 48–50.

5   Chapman, R.J. (1998) "The Role of Systems Dynamics in Understanding the Impact of Changes to Key Project Personnel on Design Production within Construction Projects", *International Journal of Project Management*, 16(4), 235–47.

less significant on the lower levels. Organisation A will be totally dependent on the environment, as clearly no organisation is divorced from its surroundings. The leadership will be tailored to the organisation and the resources will be dictated by the leadership. The systems will be devised to reflect the resources, stakeholders, leadership, organisation, environment and the other businesses within the environment.

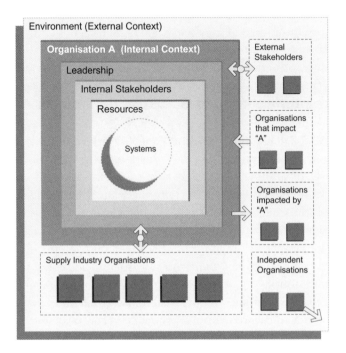

Figure 1.2   Model of ISO 31000

The seven subject areas of Figure 1.2 (namely, environment, external stakeholders [including the supply chain], organisation, leadership, internal stakeholders, risk resources and systems) have been adopted as the seven sections which subdivide this book.

The Seven Sections

- *Environment*: environment is the term used to describe an organisation's complete context, not just its natural environment. An environment is characterised by cultural, political, legal, regulatory, financial, technological, economic, developmental, environmental and social aspects. Projects will be exposed to the same aspects of the environment as the organisations which undertake them. The way in which an organisation undertakes its projects and deals with the uncertainty emanating from the environment will directly affect its health in terms of finance, reputation, stakeholder relations, repeat business, compliance and in some cases share price.

- *External stakeholders*: an external project stakeholder is a party that may influence or be influenced by a project but is not part of the organisation undertaking the project. External stakeholders are considered here to include regulators, central government agencies, local authorities, highways agencies, utility companies, design and survey consultancies, contractors, subcontractors and suppliers.

- *Organisation*: an organisation is a deliberate arrangement of people with specific roles and responsibilities, and arranged in a structure to accomplish some specific purpose. The organisation sits within an environment that influences, for instance, its purpose, structure, people, inputs, outputs, profitability and longevity. There are a number of legal types of organisations which are created in the public and private sectors.

- *Leadership*: leadership is the process of leading and influencing a group to achieve specific pre-determined goals. Leadership can occur at all levels in an organisation from board members down to individual team leaders. It is the activity undertaken by managers in leadership positions within the organisational structure. In the context of risk management, it entails agreeing the objectives for risk management, establishing a risk management function, ensuring accountability for risk management, supporting the embedding of the process and driving the implementation of improvements of risk management as part of the process of continuous improvement.

- *Internal stakeholders*: the simple definition of internal stakeholders adopted here is that they are those individuals within a project organisation who will initiate the project, sanction expenditure, agree the scope, participate in implementation and use the output. In a broader sense internal stakeholders are those who will influence the project or be affected by it. Who these stakeholders are will vary to some degree between projects in the public and private sectors and from industry to industry. The internal stakeholders of a project may include the project board, customers, end users, project managers, project teams and in-house functions such as finance, legal, information technology, public relations and human resources.

- *Resources*: risk management resources include financial, physical, human and intangible resources.

- *Systems*: "systems" is used here as a global term which includes risk management documents, software and practices. So, for instance, it includes frameworks, policies, plans, procedures and templates, hardware and software, risk management training, maturity models and risk management techniques.

Relationship between the Sections and the "Rules"

Each section contains a number of "rules" of PRM which have been selected to support the implementation of effective risk management. It would be foolhardy to claim that the rules cover all aspects of the implementation of PRM as the subject is so broad. As mentioned earlier, the "rules" are not rigid statements that have to be complied with, like those to be observed in a game of chess. They are commonly recognised "veracities" based on experience and underpinned by a combination of guidelines and recommendations included in ISO 31000, the PMI Practice Standard for Project Risk Management, the RAMP guide,[6] the PRAM Guide,[7] the Cabinet Office M_o_R Guide[8] and other notable publications, which if ignored could undermine the successful implementation of PRM. They are guidelines as projects vary so considerably, for instance, in terms of their procurement, execution, context, timeframe, complexity and scale. Included in Figure 1.3 below is a cause-and-effect diagram which illustrates the seven subject areas together with the "rules" described for each.

---

6   ICE and F&IA (1998) *Risk Analysis and Management for Projects (RAMP)*. London: Thomas Telford Publishing.
7   APM Risk Management Specific Interest Group (2010) *Project Risk Analysis and Management Guide*, 2nd edn. Princes Risborough: APM.
8   OGC (Office of Government Commerce) (2010) *Management of Risk: Guidance for Practitioners*, 3rd edn. London: The Stationery Office.

It is not intended that the book will provide an exhaustive list of "rules", but it strives to identify and describe those that are the most commonly applicable.

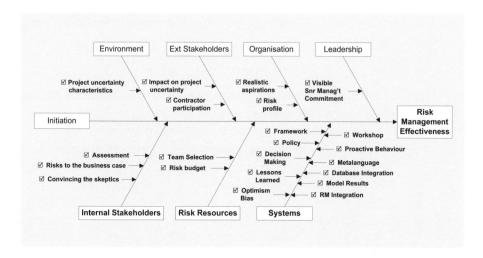

Figure 1.3 Cause-and-effect diagram of the seven subject areas and the "rules" of PRM described for each of them

2

Environment

☑ **The uncertainty characteristics of a project are the product of their origin and particularly their context**

> *This persistent global economic fragility continues to divert our attention from longer-term solutions by limiting the availability of public resources and generating greater caution in use of scarce funds for strategic investment projects.*
>
> World Economic Forum
> *("Global Risks 2013, Eighth Edition.*
> *An Initiative of the Risk Response Network")*

Projects are not created in a protective cocoon but in the wider context of their setting, which is referred to as their environment. "Environment" is the term used to describe a project's complete context, not just its natural environment. Projects implemented by private organisations are undertaken to achieve mid- to long-range goals to improve bottom-line performance. Projects undertaken in the public sector are typically undertaken to achieve socio-economic benefits. Whether a project achieves those goals will in part, as the title of this rule suggests, be dependent on its context. While it is uncommon for the aspects of a project's environment to change during the preparation of the business case, it is highly probable these aspects will be exposed to changes in their environment during execution, given that the execution of a project can span one or more years. Threats and opportunities emanating from the environment may reduce or enhance a project's business case or threaten or support its objectives.

Organisational managers must take decisions in an uncertain environment, and risk management as a discipline explicitly takes account of uncertainty and establishes how it can be addressed. The aspects of the environment described below are predominantly drawn from ISO 31000 and the definition and description of the aspects are drawn in the main from the book *Simple Tools and Techniques for Enterprise Risk Management*.[1]

Cultural

Culture can be described simply as the distinct way in which people live in different parts of the world. However, it is more than that, in that it includes the dimensions of time and region, whereby culture can be defined as an integrated system of learned behaviour patterns exhibited by the peoples which reside within a particular country. A more comprehensive description is that a culture is made up of many complex parts, such as its language(s), laws, education and health-care systems, traditions, economic and social structures (i.e. communism or capitalism), beliefs, art, music, clothing, food, currency, religion, approach to marriage, folktales and mythology. Culture is "the way of life" of a country or society and these ways of living, together with value systems, traditions and beliefs, are passed down from generation to generation. A culture can be based on different ethnic groups. For projects, culture will influence the ability to: buy or sell land and property; obtain planning, building, fire prevention and environmental approval; gain permits; use consultants and contractors from outside the country; and employ staff (recognising the local laws regarding wages, working hours, holidays, benefits and unions).

Political

Political risk may be defined as the uncertainty that stems from the exercise of power of government actors and the action of country-specific non-governmental groups. It can stem from direct government action (both regional and national) and inaction. Inaction could be the failure to issue permits, approvals or payments in a timely manner. Examples of direct action include contract frustration, import restrictions, refusal to award work permits, currency inconvertibility, tax laws, expropriation of assets or restrictions on the repatriation of profits. Nearly all projects undertaken overseas face political risk in one form or another. Political interference in

---

1   Chapman, R.J. (2011) *Simple Tools and Techniques for Enterprise Risk Management*, 2nd edn. Chichester: John Wiley & Sons. The text is either mandatory or recommended reading for university degrees in countries across the globe, including Australia, Greece, India, Malaysia, Malta, Taiwan, the UK and the USA.

projects, particularly the procurement process, is still prevalent in a number of countries where politicians seek to achieve personal gain. Such interference can lead to higher tender prices and/or tenderers with a low or inadequate technical score being selected. The political environment of overseas markets will always play a key role in shaping the threats and opportunities to the projects of businesses seeking to expand geographically. Approaches to minimise risk exposure may include investing in projects or entering into contracts where the host government has adopted policies that encourage private sector involvement (particularly where this involvement will provide risk mitigation and promote risk transfer) and has clear and unambiguous statements of government support for the type of project investment being made.

Legal

Legal risk may be defined as failing to operate within the law, failing to be aware of the laws governing project implementation, failing to maintain evidence that a project has been implemented within the law and not honouring contractual commitments or effectively managing legal risk exposure. The sources of risk that might be considered to be included within the term "legal risk" include, but not limited to, breach of environmental, copyright, human rights, health and safety, and planning legislation. In addition, this aspect may also include contract disputes, decennial liability, consequential damages and loss of reputation.

Regulatory

Regulated industries in many countries include electricity, water, gas, telecommunications, nuclear energy, pharmaceuticals, air transport, railways and ports. Changes in regulation are difficult to predict and quantify. The risk for organisations and their projects is that governments change their laws and regulations. The shifting sands of regulatory control can materially impact the business case of a project by, for example, reducing its attractiveness as an investment (due to changing government fiscal priorities), a predicted increase in operating costs or a negative change in the competitive landscape. Changes in regulation may also result in revoked licences, repudiation of a concession, retraction of technical assistance, expropriation of investor financial returns or a reduction in subsidies. Due to differences in the rate of development of renewable energy technologies, such as solar power, carbon gasification and tidal energy, there is a possibility that the evolving changes alter their respective cost ranking, which may in turn change the level of subsidies awarded to each. The very commercial viability of renewable energy projects, for instance, relies heavily on supportive regulatory regimes and financial subsidies. Renewable energy is one particular industry where governments are moving their regulatory goalposts; hence, investing in renewable energy can be a risky endeavour. In particular, wind farms have proved to be highly controversial. In the USA there have been concerns over adverse aesthetic impacts and noise pollution. Aesthetic impacts are described as reduced property values, the loss of recreational opportunities and impacts on wildlife in protected areas. In addition, the performance of wind farm turbines has been found to deteriorate more quickly than was originally envisaged.[2] A project which has suffered a delay of four years from regulatory risk is described in Case Study 1.

CASE STUDY 1 – NEW ERA WIND FARM, USA

The proposed New Era Wind Farm project is located in Goodhue County, Minnesota and consists of 48 wind turbines. The project has already been delayed by four years[1] due in the main to regulatory intervention and strong local opposition. The US Fish and Wildlife Service issued voluntary guidelines in March 2012 for developers planning wind farms called the "Land-Based Wind Energy Guidelines". Other federal agencies often interested in land-based wind project developments are the Department of Energy, the Federal Energy Regulatory Commission, and the US Department of Agriculture and its agencies. Wildlife laws and regulations that have to be complied with are numerous and include the Migratory Bird Treaty Act (MBTA), the Bald and Golden Eagle Protection Act (BGEPA) and the Endangered Species Act. In February 2013 the Minnesota Public Utilities Commission (PUC) decided to re-examine the

---

1   Marcotty, Josephine (2013) "Eagles Win a Round as PUC Delays Wind Farm near Red Wing", *Star Tribune*, 28 February.

---

2   Research into the performance of wind farms published by the Renewable Energy Foundation (recorded in its 2012 publication "The Performance of Wind Farms in the UK and Denmark", written by Gordon Hughes) has demonstrated an unambiguous and statistically significant decline in the operating performance of wind farms as they grow older. Fall off in performance is happening far quicker than previously envisaged. Two plausible explanations are offered. The first is that turbines are becoming less efficient over time as a result of mechanical wear and tear, erosion of turbine blades and related factors. Secondly, the turbines experience more frequent breakdowns and their operators are slow to bring them back into service.

Goodhue Wind Project given the changes in the ownership structure, financing, date of service and the operating elements of the project.[2] The conflict between the two opposing environmental goals – clean energy and the protection of wildlife – is on the increase as wind farm proposals "pop up" across the country. On the one hand, state law requires that utilities derive 25 per cent of their energy from wind by 2020. On the other hand, there is growing realisation that the massive towers and their rapidly travelling blades are killing thousands of bats and birds each year. This problem becomes more prominent or acute when the birds in jeopardy are endangered species.

---

2 "Minnesota Public Utilities Commission Re-opens the Goodhue Wind Project in Light of Changes", press release, 28 February 2013.

Financial

An aspect of the environment is project finance. For larger projects, an organisation may seek external support to finance a project or programme (group) of projects. The availability, cost and contract terms engaged in to secure the finance will be influenced by other aspects of the environment, such as the economy and legislation applied to the finance sector. The consideration of raising project finance will involve an examination of potential movement in material, transportation, energy, fuel, labour and tender prices (which can increase disproportionately due to the volume of work underway at any one time). In addition, consideration will be given to inflation, operating costs, borrowing costs, payback periods and taxation. Sometimes investors and contractual participants assume certain risks in return for an opportunity to share in the project's upside potential. Tracking accounts are often used to compensate input suppliers or offtakers for offering fixed-price agreements, which shield project sponsors from market risk. Under an offtake agreement that provides for tracking, if the contract price exceeds spot market prices, the difference between the two would be tracked. Equity kickers, such as convertible debentures, stock warrants and contingent interest payments, allow investors to share in the upside potential of the project while still giving them priority over common equity investors with regard to claims on project assets and cashflow if the project is unable to generate sufficient cashflow to meet its financial obligations. Of the many contractual structures that can allocate risks during the operating period, take-or-pay[3] and put-or-pay are perhaps the most commonly applied.

---

3 *Take-or-pay* arrangements require the offtaker to pay for the goods or service regardless of whether it is needed. This obligation is normally conditioned on, among other things, the project's

Technological

Technological risk may be defined as events that would lead to insufficient, inappropriate or mismanaged investment in technology, in terms of manufacturing processes, product design, technology maturity and/or information management. To put this definition into context, it is necessary to understand what is meant by technology. The economist's perspective of technology is that it is a component of capital goods (one of the factors of production) used by businesses to produce commodities consumed by society. From this viewpoint, technology is a subset of production, the process that transforms inputs into a set of outputs. Traditionally this means turning raw materials and component parts into finished goods. While technology is important to the process of production, its application is broader. The *Oxford Everyday Dictionary* definition is as follows: "technology is the scientific study of mechanical arts and applied sciences". Mechanical arts and the sciences are continuously applied to product design. Hence, products exhibit incremental advances in technology and their functionality, quality and reliability influence market creation, market share and market growth. Projects are often implemented to take advantage of new technology for competitive advantage, to match progress already made by competitors or simply for operational benefits. As such, technology is often embraced for economic reasons. Emerging technologies generally (and not specific to construction) include nanotechnology, cloning, eugenics, smart materials, cloud computing and services, and the mobile Internet. Construction technology may include advances in existing technologies such as barcodes, robotics, global positioning and modular prefabrication. The adoption of novel technology is inherently risky, but may provide those less risk averse with substantial competitive advantages. Case Study 2 below is an example of a project not achieving its objectives due to its inability to successfully incorporate novel technology.

---

compliance with the terms of the offtake or concession agreement. Payments under take-or-pay contracts may be set to cover all fixed costs of the project (fixed operation and maintenance costs, debt service, after-tax equity return) or may cover only part of the project's available capacity. In the latter case, project sponsors must sell the uncommitted portion to the spot market or seek long-term offtake arrangements with third parties to achieve their required equity return.

CASE STUDY 2 – NEW DENVER INTERNATIONAL AIRPORT, USA

The City and County of Denver built the New Denver International Airport, which extends over 13,568 hectares (about 53 square miles), with three parallel north-south runways, two parallel east-west runways and room for a total of 12 major runways. It cost approximately $4.9 billion. Despite the City of Denver being advised by architects and airlines alike that proceeding with a technologically sophisticated airport-wide automated baggage-handling system posed a high risk in terms of not meeting the airport's scheduled October 1993 opening date, it decided to accept the risk.[1] BAE Automated Systems Incorporated was awarded a $193 million contract to design, build and test an automated baggage-handling system.[2] The system was originally designed to distribute all baggage (including transfers) automatically between check-in and the aircraft and then with pick-up on arrival. The system employed novel technology and was unique in terms of both its complexity and capacity.[3] It was recognised that the successful operation of the airport as a hub hinged on the speed of baggage handling to achieve acceptable boarding and transfer times at Denver, where the distances involved were much greater than those at other airports. Its owners had marketed the airport to the airlines as a highly efficient platform for hub operations because of its planned ability to turn around aircraft flights very rapidly. United Airlines, the dominant airline at Denver, insisted on a rapid baggage-handling system before signing its lease with Denver.[4] The Denver system was therefore originally designed to deliver bags much faster than current norms at major airports at up to 38 km/h (24 mph).[5] The maximum delivery time was apparently set at 20 minutes for narrow body aircraft and 30 minutes for wide body aircraft. However, despite knowing the central importance of the automated baggage system, its detailed design was not integrated with the building design and was only commenced after construction of the airport was underway and only some two years before the airport was planned to open. The promised access dates for BAE were not achieved. As a consequence of its late commencement, it suffered from inadequate space for the baggage-handling installation and time for completion. This schedule precluded extensive simulation or physical testing of the full baggage-handling design. As a result of the problems with the fully automated baggage-handling system, the project was completed 16 months

1   US GAO (1995) "Denver International Airport: Baggage Handling, Contracting, and Other Issues", United States General Accounting Office, fact sheet for the Honourable Hank Brown, US Senate.
2   US GAO (1994) "Denver International Airport: Impact of the Delayed Baggage System", United States General Accounting Office, fact sheet for the Honourable Hank Brown, US Senate, GAO/RCED-95-35BR.
3   De Neufville, R. (1994) "The Baggage System at Denver: Prospects and Lessons", *Journal of Air Transport Management*, 1(4), 229–36.
4   Swartz, J.A. (1996) "Airport 95: Automated Baggage System?" *Software Engineering Notes*, 21(2), 79–83.
5   US GAO (1994) "Denver International Airport: Impact of the Delayed Baggage System".

late. To achieve an acceptable level of functionality, the system had to be scaled back in terms of its complexity and performance. Automation never worked for incoming flights, whose baggage has been moved by handlers from the time of the opening of the airport. In addition, no airline other than United Airlines tried to use the error-prone system.[6] The cost of the baggage-handling system increased from $193 million to over $290 million,[7] which was largely passed on to the airlines serving the airport.

6   Johnson, K. (2005) "Denver Airport Saw the Future. It Didn't Work", *New York Times*, 27 August 2005 .
7   US GAO (1995) "Denver International Airport: Baggage Handling, Contracting, and Other Issues".

Case Study 3 below is based on the West Coast Main Line in the UK, which is a clear example of where the introduction of new technology on a major railway introduced considerable uncertainty and major threats to programme delivery. The National Audit Office[4] argued that only by reducing the technology risk through reliance on conventional signalling (for most of the railway upgrade) and by tightening controls, particularly over changes to scope, were the Strategic Rail Authority and Network Rail (which replaced Railtrack in October 2002) able to turn the programme round. The programme had run into considerable difficulties in terms of both cost and time. Abortive costs exceeded £350 million. The scale of the project was considerable given its geographical reach. Perhaps the significance of the railway line to the UK can be best appreciated by the fact that the route carries over 2,000 train movements each day and is used for more than 75 million rail journeys each year.[5]

4   National Audit Office (NAO) (2006) *The Modernisation of the West Coast Main Line*, Report by the Comptroller and Auditor General, HC 22 Session 2006–2007, 22 November. London: The Stationery Office.
5   RailwayPeople.com: http://www.railwaypeople.com/rail-projects/west-coast-route-modernisation -3.html; ATOC: http://www.atoc.org/media-centre/previous-press-releases/west-coast-works-gather -pace-in-scotland-100318.

CASE STUDY 3 – WEST COAST ROUTE MODERNISATION, UK

The West Coast Main Line (WCML) railway line runs from London Euston to Glasgow Central for approximately 650 km, with diverging routes to Birmingham, Manchester, Manchester Airport, Liverpool and Edinburgh. The WCML (with its origins in the 1830s) is one of the busiest mixed rail traffic routes in Europe. In June 1998 the Rail Regulator[1] gave approval to the commercial agreement[2] between the Virgin Rail Group (the operator of the West Coast passenger rail franchise) and Railtrack (the private sector owner-operator of the rail infrastructure) to upgrade services on the WCML. The project involved the acquisition of new high-speed rolling stock by Virgin and major investment in the WCML by Railtrack. The project was to be implemented in two phases. Phase 1 planned to provide higher-frequency services and reduce journey times through the introduction of tilting trains and an improvement in line speeds from 110 mph to 125 mph by 2002, and Phase 2 planned to increase line speeds up to 140 mph by 2005. To achieve the higher train speeds of 140 mph (and to comply with EC Directive 96/48/EC),[3] Railtrack initially decided to adopt moving block signalling (level 3 ERTMS).[4, 5] In December 1999, finding the technology to be insufficiently developed, Railtrack abandoned level 3 and adopted level 2 ERTMS, but still needed to achieve the 140 mph running specified in PUG2. Railtrack estimated the cost of level 2 ERTMS for the WCML at £1.9 billion, as it would need to replace conventional signalling. In June 2002 the Strategic Rail Authority (SRA) convened an industry-wide workshop[6] which recommended that ERTMS be removed from the WCML programme. In addition, the SRA Strategy recommended the removal of the Network Management Centre, on which Railtrack had already spent £350 million. These recommendations were accepted, for at the time it was considered prudent to accept this level of loss rather than be exposed to far greater losses in the future. Continued ERTMS development work, to address European Union requirements, was transferred

---

1   ORR Approval to PUG 2: http://www.rail-reg.gov.uk/server/show/ConWebDoc.5800.
2   The agreement was known as the Passenger Upgrade Agreement (PUG2) agreement.
3   Directive 96/48/EC requires Member States to operate compatible signalling systems for upgrades of high-speed lines on the European network.
4   ERTMS is the acronym for the European Rail Traffic Management System, which is an initiative backed by the European Union to enhance cross-border interoperability and the procurement of signalling equipment by creating a single Europe-wide standard for train control-and-command systems. The two main components of ERTMS are the European Train Control System (ETCS), a standard for in-cab train control, and GSM-R, the GSM mobile communications standard for railway operations. The equipment can be further subdivided between on-board and infrastructure equipment.
5   Level 1: equivalent to the Train Protection Warning System but using newer technology; Level 2: involves in-cab (as opposed to lineside) signalling, with instructions sent to the cab by GSM radio; Level 3: as for Level 2, but with remotely operating points and self-reporting trains which can increase the capacity and improve the performance of the routes.
6   NAO (2006) *The Modernisation of the West Coast Main Line, Report by the Comptroller and Auditor General*, HC 22 Session 2006–2007, 22 November. London: The Stationery Office.

to a national ERTMS development programme. In January 2003 the Health and Safety Commission accepted the SRA's advice that ERTMS was not sufficiently reliable for the WCML and was a major risk to programme delivery, and the Project Board approved its removal from the programme. It was considered that going forward on this simpler basis, the project would become more efficient and less prone to the effects of technological risk on costs, timescales and outputs.

Economic

Economic risk may be defined as "the influence of national macroeconomics on the performance of an individual business" (recognising that while national macroeconomics will be the dominating influence on individual businesses, the UK economy is heavily influenced by the ongoing Eurozone crisis). Implicit within national macroeconomics is the modifying influence of government policy through the manipulation of aggregate demand and consumer spending. While governments cannot create economic growth on their own, they can create the conditions for business success. The current UK government is looking to stimulate growth through a number of initiatives, such as striving to establish domestic economic stability,[6] supporting initiatives in the G7, G20 and the EU to secure international economic stability, modifying corporation tax, protecting intellectual property, providing access to finance for small and medium enterprises (SMEs) and attracting investment within the UK. In specific response to the uncertainty around the delivery of projects, the UK government has the ability to change planning legislation, government procurement processes, the cost of capital and the extent of government investment in infrastructure. The current UK government has established initiatives to look at reducing the cost of construction, identify barriers to innovation in construction and improve the efficiency of the supply chain. However, due to the remaining fragility of the global economic markets, projected slow annual growth and current UK debt levels, government spending will continue to be constrained.[7]

---

6   The UK's structural fiscal position was one of the best in the G7 in 2000, but by 2007, just before the crisis, had deteriorated to be the worst in the G7. Following the recent financial crisis, only the US faced a larger structural fiscal deficit than the UK. See HM Treasury (2010) *The Path to Strong Sustainable and Balanced Growth*, available at: http://webarchive.nationalarchives. gov.uk/+/http://www.bis.gov.uk/assets/biscore/corporate/docs/p/pu1099-path-to-strong-sustainable-and-balanced-growth.pdf.

7   World Economic Forum (2013) "Global Risks 2013", 8th edn, available at: http://www3. weforum.org/docs/WEF_GlobalRisks_Report_2013.pdf.

Environmental

Environmental risk for projects has many facets and can take many forms. Environmental risk can relate to an adverse impact of a project on its neighbouring environment, such as an oil spill, or an adverse impact on the project by an act of nature, such as fires, floods, high winds, volcanic ash, tsunamis or hurricanes. Projects may also be exposed to increased project costs arising from more onerous environmental legislation ("red tape"), project-specific approval conditions or increased project durations arising from the time taken to obtain approval. Project owners may receive fines or penalties arising from breaches of legislation and disasters caused by projects. Organisations may suffer from reputational risk . when they attract adverse publicity relating to an environmental incident (or the subsequent handling of an incident).

Developmental

In pursuit of business growth through geographical expansion, organisations frequently implement projects overseas. The extent to which a country has experienced developmental growth will influence the ease with which a new project can be implemented and subsequently operated. A way of understanding and describing the differences in development experienced by different countries is by subdividing them into groups. Perhaps the most well-known groups are labelled "developing" and "developed". According to the United Nations Statistics Division, there is no established convention for the designation of developing and developed countries. The individual approaches adopted by the United Nations Development Programme (UNDP), the World Bank and the International Monetary Fund (IMF) to the construction of a classification system to describe a country's development attainment are very different (including, for instance, the choice of terminology). Nonetheless, their taxonomies are similar in that they have assessed about 20–25 per cent of countries as being developed. The group of developing countries is therefore large and all three institutions have found it useful to identify subgroups among developing countries. Less developed countries are characterised as having poor medical services, housing and public transportation, as well as unsafe water supplies and exposure to interruption to power supplies. In addition, the degree of development is measured by the literacy of the population, salaries and life expectancy.

Social

The social aspect of a business' or project's context is addressed by ISO 31000. Social risk for projects may be defined as the qualities and characteristics of the local workforce in terms of their education, health, skills, work ethic, linguistic capabilities, religion and attitude to crime, safety and pollution. For projects completed by an organisation in its native country, the social aspect of the environment may not warrant special attention. However, when being implemented in undeveloped countries, social aspects will come to the fore very quickly. Social aspects will feature alongside local employment laws, particularly those regarding the employment of foreign nationals, taxation, health screening, work permits and visas.

Context

Each of the ten aspects of a project's environment described above may be a source of potential threat to a project's objectives. For each of the ten aspects, six examples have been identified which may increase project uncertainty. These examples are listed in Table 2.1 below. This is far from an exhaustive list; it is purely an indication of potential sources of threats (and opportunities) that may warrant closer scrutiny. Legal and environmental factors for instance may be very considerable. In addition, due to the correlation between aspects of the environment such as financial and economic as well as regulatory and environmental, care must be taken not to duplicate factors.

Table 2.1   Potential threats emanating from a project's environment

Aspect	Factor	Aspect	Factor
Cultural	Public holidays	**Technological**	Nanotechnology
	Hours of working		Robotic devices
	Mandatory staff benefits		Modular prefabrication
	Languages		Disassembly and reuse
	Religion and prayer time		Global positioning systems
	Permits and approvals		Seamless supply chains
Political	Permits	**Economic**	Inflation
	Contract frustration		Exchange rates
	Import restrictions		Interest rates
	Currency inconvertibility		Import duties/restrictions
	Expropriation of assets		Labour market (manpower availability)
	Asset repatriation restrictions		Change in material and equipment prices
Legal	Planning law	**Environmental**	Protected species – animals and birds
	Environmental law		Climate change
	Health and Safety law		Wildlife and countryside
	Consumer protection law		Disposal of contaminated land
	Human rights law		Hazardous waste
	Copyright law		Pollution – air, land and water
Regulatory	Environment (all industries)	**Developmental**	Salaries
	Planning (all industries)		Health care
	Specific industry (i.e. nuclear)		Water supplies
	Data protection		Transportation
	Employment		Power supplies
	Health & sSafety (all industries)		Life expectancy
Financial	Sources of funding	**Social**	Crime
	Lending rates		Language barriers
	Payback periods		Health culture and screening
	Change in prices		Attitude to alcohol and drugs
	Taxation, VAT		Employment of foreign nationals
	Prices		Welfare support

A project's environment will introduce uncertainty from each of its aspects.

3

External Project Stakeholders

☑ **Project success requires comprehension of the potential impact of external stakeholders on project uncertainty**

> *The most important issues that risk management helps to resolve are usually related to objectives and relationships between project parties.*
> Chapman, C. and Ward, S. (2003)
> Project Risk Management, Processes, Techniques and Insights,
> *2nd edn. Chichester: John Wiley & Sons*

An axiom of project execution is that external stakeholders have the ability to significantly increase project uncertainty. Their actions can be positive or negative and hence they can enhance or undermine project performance. In the case where performance is adversely affected, stakeholders can erode the ability to realise the project objectives and in extreme cases can invalidate the business case. It should also be noted that overlooked stakeholders can result in design rework and at worst construction rework. Recognition of this project "given" calls for a systematic approach to external stakeholder management involving the steps of identification, analysis, mapping and ultimately management, as illustrated in Figure 3.1 below. The optimum solution is to maximise the benefits to be derived from stakeholders and to minimise (or hopefully neutralise) the negative impacts. The focus of this rule of PRM is on the analysis and mapping steps and in particular on gaining an understanding of the potential impact that these stakeholders may have on outturn project performance. Comprehension of the impact of stakeholder behaviour entails predicting the likelihood, nature, timing and extent of stakeholder actions.

Figure 3.1   Stakeholder management process steps

There would appear to be no consistent definition of external project stakeholders in the literature. The definition adopted here is that an external project stakeholder is a party that may influence or be influenced by a project, but is not part of the organisation for which the project is undertaken. An external project stakeholder may be a company such as a firm of solicitors that is engaged to supply services, a bank that provides funding or a local authority that provides planning approval for development.

Identification

The first step in the stakeholder management process is to identify who the stakeholders are. While the majority of stakeholders may be immediately apparent, unless identification is proactively managed, stakeholders may emerge over time and may potentially be very disruptive. An often-cited approach to identification is to use the brainstorming technique; however, while this encourages free thinking, unless it is used in conjunction with stimuli, it may not live up to initial expectations in terms of productivity. Clearly, consideration needs to be given to those stakeholders who would have the power to stop the project, amend its scope or alter its timing. In addition, there should be deliberation over those who could influence it or who would be affected by it. Ideally, those conducting stakeholder analyses should think beyond the obvious, such as giving consideration to secondary stakeholders. The identification of external stakeholders to a construction project, for instance, can be accomplished by considering one or more of the following eight perspectives:

- *Economy*: viewing a project as being part of a local economy. This may prompt thoughts about local businesses, employment, tourism, transport, environment, urban planning, housing and health care.

- *Process*: considering the processes that stakeholders will be involved in, such as funding, regulating, advising, planning, designing, approving, contracting and supplying.

- *Location*: reflecting on the context of the project in terms of its location, such as whether it is in an area of high urban density, conservation, regeneration or countryside.

- *Industry*: considering the types of construction project and the unique stakeholders each project will have. For instance, projects involving pharmaceutical buildings, nuclear plants, coal-fired power stations, oil refineries, prisons, airports and new railways will have stakeholders specific to the industry to which they belong.

- *Similar projects*: speaking to participants in similar ongoing or completed projects.

- *Stakeholders*: speaking to stakeholders identified early on in the process to obtain their views.

- *Media*: consulting the media (post-confidentiality agreement).

- *Stage*: examining the stakeholders involved in each of the project life cycle (PLC) stages and intervening gate reviews, recognising that a stakeholder may be involved in or affect multiple stages. Included in Table 3.1 below is an example of the PLC of a simple construction project where the stakeholders have been identified against the project stages.

Table 3.1   Using a PLC to identify stakeholders

Inception →	Business Case →	Design →	Procurement →	Execution →	Handover
Sponsor	Sponsor	Sponsor	Sponsor	Sponsor	Sponsor
Financial adviser	Bank(s)	Designers	Consultants	Neighbours	Consultants
Key customers	Financial adviser(s)	Consultants	Legal adviser	Community groups	Local authority
Key shareholders	Legal adviser	Subconsultants	Contractors	Local authority	Contractor(s)
	Central government	Subcontractors providing design	Subcontractors	Utility companies	Subcontractor(s)
	Local authority	Land agent	Suppliers	Insurance broker	Operator
	Customers	Operator	Insurer	Insurance company	Insurer
	Competitors	Local authority	Media	Media	Media
	Regulator	Neighbours		Social networking – websites	
	Shareholders	Community groups		Police	
	Designer			General public	
	Consultants			Contractor(s)	
	Land agent			Subcontractors	
				Suppliers	
				Operator	

Analysis

The second step in the stakeholder management process is analysis. Stakeholder analysis is a strategic tool since it attempts to answer questions such as: what are the stakeholders' interests in the project? What degree of power does each possess? At what stage in the PLC would they interface with the project? Will they be supportive or in direct opposition to the project? Will they attempt to corral and persuade others of their position? Will they undermine the business case for the project and render it unviable or will they be staunch advocates and strengthen the business case? Analysis is critical to understanding the potential sources of uncertainty, the degree of that uncertainty, what form the uncertainty might take (such as application rejection by the local . planning authority, delayed environmental approval, legal challenges by neighbouring businesses or residents, or adverse media coverage) and the type of proactive action (or response) that should be followed.

Interests

Stakeholder interests can be many and varied. A few of the more common ones are as follows:

- *Environment*: protection of open space and wildlife, conservation of resources, concerns over noise, air and sound pollution, deforestation and climate change.

- *Economics*: improvement in or deterioration of job opportunities, increased imports, reduced exports or changes in standards of living.

- *Adjoining owners*: noise, dust, increase in traffic, increase in crime, increase or devaluation of property prices.

- *Countryside*: protection of views, tourism, country life, natural habitats and protected species.

External Stakeholders with "High" Power

There are a number of areas of project implementation where external stakeholders have the power to halt, delay, change a project or increase its price:

- *Sponsor*: a sponsor's hierarchy of decision making, committee processes, lack of delegated authority or lack of awareness of the need for expeditious decisions can create delays.

- *Funder*: a bank's refusal to provide funding (or the recall of an existing loan) may halt a project until an alternative funding source can be found. In addition, a bank's requirement for specific repayment terms or levels of interest which exceed expectations may necessitate a re-evaluation of the business case and/or necessitate establishing alternative funding arrangements. Even when a funding agreement is in place, the release of funds may be slower than anticipated and may delay project commencement. An example of a project that required strong stakeholder management from a funding perspective is the Eden project described in Case Study 4.

- *Landowner*: negotiations to conclude the purchase of a site may outstrip expectations.

- *Environmental agency*: an environmental agency may significantly delay commencement through its approval processes, impose unexpected and costly conditions and/or stop the work in progress if it considers the project to be in breach of pre-existing conditions. An example of this is given in Case Study 6.

- *Planning authority*: like an environmental agency, a planning authority may delay approval, impose conditions which may attract additional costs and/or time and stop work if the granted approval conditions are breached. An example of a project that required strong stakeholder management from a building approval perspective is the Water Cube project described in Case Study 5.

- *Contracted parties*: the poor performance and/or integration of designers, contractors, subcontractors or suppliers may delay a project and may lead to additional costs. The sheer scale of the task of managing the interfaces between designers and contractors can be a determining factor in whether a project meets its objectives. Case Study 6 describes the "Big Dig" project, which had a myriad of stakeholders to manage, a fact that was singled out as a contributor to poor project performance.

- *Port authority*: import restrictions or port delays may impact a project's outturn completion date.

- *Utility companies*: the poor performance of utility companies can be particularly problematic in terms of approving drawings or completing works. In addition, the poor accuracy of utility company drawings can be highly disruptive. Drawings may show utilities that were never installed or completed utilities in the wrong location or at the wrong depth. Perhaps more problematic are the completed utilities that have not been recorded and are damaged by the contractor during the course of the work. An example of this is given in Case Study 6.

CASE STUDY 4 – THE EDEN PROJECT, UK

The Eden Project is located in a reclaimed china clay quarry at Bodelva near St Austell in Cornwall. The site area covers 15 hectares. The project is an internationally renowned environmental centre and visitor attraction, the brainchild of Tim Smit (Chief Executive of Eden Project Limited), who was already famous for his involvement in the restoration of the Lost Gardens of Heligan. At the Museums Association Conference and Exhibition in Brighton 2011, Smit urged museums and galleries to modernise and take more risks to realise opportunities. He said: "most people who don't take risks don't know, but taking risks only seems huge until you take them. After that all the energy you spend on being afraid goes into the project instead".[1] Project success only occurred as a result of substantial stakeholder management effort, which was required in the main due to the number of public and private funders involved. Davis Langdon records that stakeholder management was a conscious activity and that "key issues including the management of stakeholders were explicitly addressed in the Project Management Plan".[2] As of February 2009, investment in the project totalled £132.382 million, with some 36.5 per cent coming from the public sector, 42.8 per cent from the Millennium Commission and the balance of 20.7 per cent from the private sector. The funders included the Millennium Commission, the South West Regional Development Agency (SWRDA), the European Regional Development Fund (ERDF), English Partnerships, Cornwall County Council, Restormel Borough Council, the Royal Bank of Scotland and

---

1   Museums Association (2011) "Smit Tells Museums to Take Risks", 3 October, http://www. museumsassociation.org/news/03102011-tim-smit.
2   Building.co.uk (2006) "Success Projects", http://www.building.co.uk/data/successful-projects /3062420.article.

other public and private bodies in the UK and Europe.[3] Smit described managing the funding of the Eden Project as "herding eels".[4] The first bid to the Millennium Commission was rejected and two further submissions were then made, each reducing the capital costs.[5] In the spring of 2001, a structured finance deal was agreed with the Royal Bank of Scotland, which David Maneer (Marketing Director of the Eden Project) described as extraordinarily complex and which essentially involved leasing parts of the site and plant in order to liberate funds.

3   Amion Consulting Ltd (2009) "Evaluation of the Eden Project and SWRDA's Role", final report, February.
4   http://www.insights.org.uk/articleitem.aspx?title=The+Eden+Project.
5   "Some Interesting Facts and Milestones", http://www.cornishspirit.co.uk/Deutsch/eden_facts_de.htm.

Analysis:
Likelihood of Occurrence and the Impact of Stakeholder Behaviour

For stakeholder management to be effective and, in particular, for management effort to be focused in order to achieve the greatest returns, a project needs to have a clear understanding of those stakeholders that may pose the greatest risk to securing the project's objectives. A way of accomplishing this is to identify and analyse the potential risk events associated with each stakeholder. Analysis will entail where in the PLC the stakeholders will be involved in the project, which specific activities they will be engaged in and their past behaviour (such as conditions imposed by planning authorities and the environment agency). Assessing the activities of a stakeholder, their timing and potential impact will entail understanding a number of things about the project, such as the prioritised (and ideally weighted) project objectives, the execution plan, the project scope, the procurement route (and the consequential PLC sequence of project stages), the baseline programme and the cost plan.

These documents will enable the project to determine:

- which activities will be affected;

- at what stage in the programme a stakeholder may delay the project or cause costs to rise;

- the sensitivity of a potential delay of one activity on the overall outturn project duration; and

- the interconnectedness of different stakeholders in terms of their sequential (or parallel) impact on the programme.

Likelihood

The likelihood that a stakeholder will negatively affect a project will be influenced by the following factors:

- How well defined the stakeholder's internal decision-making processes are (such as those of a central government sponsored regulator).

- The typical length of the decision-making process (such as that taken by a local authority planning department).

- The number of steps in the decision-making process.

- Whether the stakeholder's actions will be governed by legislation and hence can be predicted to a degree.

- The latitude that a stakeholder has in the interpretation of national regulations/legislation (such as a local authority building regulation department).

- How long the stakeholder has been established and whether its membership and objectives are evolving (such as a community group).

Impact

In addition, analysis will be required with regard to the impact of identified risk events. Figure 3.2 below illustrates a simple probability impact grid for the measures of project success, described in this example as time, cost and quality. Clearly, the measures of success and the range of impacts selected must be tailored to suit each project. In Figure 3.2, five scales of impact have been selected for each measure of success. Each scale is expressed as a band – for example, a high "time" impact is expressed as higher than 12 weeks and less than or equal to 16 weeks. The probability of a risk will be same for each measure of success; however, a risk may have no cost impact, a low-quality impact and a very high time impact.

Probability		Time: Very Low > 0 ≤ 4 Wks	Low > 4 Wks ≤ 8 Wks	Med > 8 Wks ≤ 12 Wks	High > 12 Wks ≤ 16 Wks	Very High > 16 Wks
Very High	> 75%	5	10	15	20	25
High	> 50% ≤ 75%	4	8	12	16	20
Med	> 25% ≤ 50%	3	6	9	12	15
Low	> 5% ≤ 25%	2	4	6	8	10
Very Low	< 5%	1	2	3	4	5

Probability		Cost: Very Low > 0 ≤ $5 million	Low > $5 million ≤ $10 million	Med > $10 million ≤ $15 million	High > $15 million ≤ $20 million	Very High > $20 million
Very High	> 75%	5	10	15	20	25
High	> 50% ≤ 75%	4	8	12	16	20
Med	> 25% ≤ 50%	3	6	9	12	15
Low	> 5% ≤ 25%	2	4	6	8	10
Very Low	< 5%	1	2	3	4	5

Probability		Quality: Very Low Full Business Case not achieved	Low Core project objective not achieved	Med Scope not fully achieved	High Major shortfall in achievement of specification	Very High Minor shortfall in achievement of specification
Very High	> 75%	5	10	15	20	25
High	> 50% ≤ 75%	4	8	12	16	20
Med	> 25% ≤ 50%	3	6	9	12	15
Low	> 5% ≤ 25%	2	4	6	8	10
Very Low	< 5%	1	2	3	4	5

Figure 3.2 Project probability impact grid

It should be borne in mind that this grid is merely an example and will not be appropriate for many projects in terms of, for instance, those that have more project objectives, those that wish to give a weighting to probability or impacts and those that wish to carry out quantitative analysis (where the desire is to model impacts that do not sit exactly within one of the impact scales, i.e. if the desire is to model a time impact which may fall between 4 and 16 weeks).

Mapping

Frequently cited within the organisational literature is Mitchell et al.'s paper,[1] which describes a theory of stakeholder identification and salience, and in particular a classification of stakeholders. Mitchell et al.'s typology[2] of stakeholders within a firm's environment could be considered for projects implemented by firms. In particular, the paper states that some stakeholders will possess what it calls the urgency attribute, which is the claim for immediate attention. This is particularly important for projects which have specific start and end dates, interim milestones and typically finite resources. Care must be

1 Mitchell, R.K. Bradley, R.A. and Wood, D.J. (1997) "Toward a Theory of Stakeholder Identification and Salience: Defining the Principle of Who and What Really Counts", *Academy of Management Review*, 22(4), 853–86.

2 Typology refers to a systematic classification of types that have characteristics or traits in common.

taken to respond promptly to stakeholders that warrant a quick response to maintain the schedule rather than those that shout the loudest. A description of the typology is described in Appendix F.

While there is significant preoccupation with stakeholder mapping in the literature, what practical benefit does it offer? Stakeholder mapping assists project team members to analyse stakeholder in terms of predicting their behaviour (based on the assumption that stakeholders are generally true to type). In addition, stakeholder mapping supports classifying stakeholders as well as assisting in defining the type of relationship to be developed, where management effort should be prioritised and potential approaches to stakeholder management.

The Power/Interest Matrix

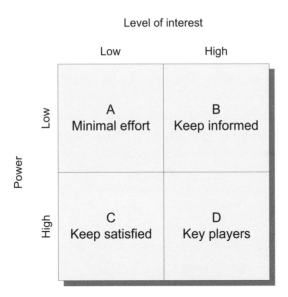

Figure 3.3   **Stakeholder groups based on Mendelow's[3] power/interest matrix**

---

3   Mendelow, A. (1991) *Proceedings of the 2nd International Conference on Information Systems,* Cambridge, MA.

A way of mapping stakeholder characteristics is the power/interest matrix (composed of four zones representing distinct stakeholder groups), as shown in Figure 3.3. The groups are labelled A to D for ease of reference. This classifies stakeholders in relation to the power that they hold and their level of interest in the project. The type of relationship which a project will need to establish and maintain with each type of stakeholder group is shown for each of the four zones. Stakeholders with little interest in the project activities and little power to influence them (Zone A) will require *minimal effort* on the part of the project team. Those stakeholders with a high level of interest in the project's activities but little power to influence them (Zone B) will need to be *kept informed* of the major decisions which have been made. Hence, regular informative communication with this group is required. Stakeholders in the other two zones warrant and will require a greater degree of attention. Clearly, the acceptability of decisions to the *key players* in Zone D is a major consideration when developing, for instance, the project's business case, together with the project's communication, execution and risk management plans. However, of all of the groups, the stakeholders in Zone C are the most difficult to manage. Their level of interest in an organisation's activities or projects will remain low as long as they are *kept satisfied* and agree with the decisions adopted. However, if they become dissatisfied, then because of their powerful position, they can easily increase their interest and move to Zone D, thus becoming key players. This group may be landowners whose property is being possessed through compulsory purchase orders (and who have sought judicial review), businesses that have agreed to vacate their premises to make way for a project (but that will seek legal redress if they believe the contract terms are being breached) or local community organisations (that challenge planning decisions).

CASE STUDY 5 – THE WATER CUBE, BEIJING[1]

The National Aquatics Centre (colloquially known as the Water Cube) was built as the swimming venue for the 2008 Beijing Olympic Games. In July 2003 the Water Cube design was chosen from 10 proposals submitted in an international architectural competition. The project was subsequently designed and built by a consortium composed of PTW Architects (an Australian architecture

---

1   This case study is based on the APM Project Management Awards, "Winner's Case Study", Category: Overseas Project of the Year 2008; Winner: Arup for The Water Cube, Beijing, available at: http://www.apm.org.uk/sites/default/files/tmp/APM%20Awards%20Case%20 Studies.pdf.

firm), Arup international engineering group, CSCEC (China State Construction Engineering Corporation) and CCDI (China Construction Design International) of Shanghai. It was handed over for occupation on time (28 January 2008) and also within budget. One of the primary contributing factors to its success was the management of stakeholders by the Arup project management team. With the aim of establishing a planned approach to the project, combined with their concerns over trying to predict the project's risk exposure, Arup's project management team sought to develop an understanding of the project's complex and unfamiliar context. This entailed gaining an insight into the project's environment through examining its legal, social, cultural, economic and technological components in order to avoid underestimating the risks associated with delivering the Water Cube. To this end, the team held specific internal sessions with Chinese team members to quickly establish an approach. These sessions focused on looking at how to minimise and manage the risks of the specific differences in norms, practices and expectations across the PLC. Beijing's lack of regulatory transparency and regional differences as well as a relationship-based business culture were among the factors Arup identified that made China a challenging project environment. The key risks identified related to how the external stakeholders would be involved in approving the design concept. Some of the challenges faced included the integration and the coordination of the many interfaces of the project involving multiple stakeholders with conflicting demands. Coordinating the requirements for athletes, officials, VIPs, the media, broadcasters, the workforce, sponsors, spectators and of course the operator was a complex process and required a delicate balance to be struck.

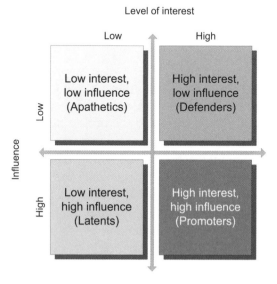

Figure 3.4   World Bank categorisations of risk

The World Bank's Approach to Stakeholder Mapping

Another way of categorising external stakeholders is proposed by the World Bank,[4] which is illustrated in Figure 3.4. The World Bank uses four attributes within a matrix to organise and classify stakeholder data, which are labelled "Promoters", "Defenders", "Latents" and "Apathetics". These categories may strike a chord with those experienced in participating in projects. The definition of these four different categories as interpreted for projects is as follows:

- *Promoters*: stakeholders who have great interest in the project and help to make it successful.

- *Defenders*: stakeholders who have a vested interest in the project and can voice their support in the community or with the aid of the media, but who have little actual power to influence the effort in any way.

- *Latents*: stakeholders whose have no particular interest or involvement in the project, but who have the power to influence it greatly if they became interested.

- *Apathetics*: stakeholders who have little interest and little power, and who may even not know that the project exists.

Management

More and more projects are developing a communication plan which contains a description of the means and frequency of communication between the external stakeholders and the project team. As a minimum, the communication plan will contain a list of the external stakeholders, the points of contact in each, the information to be supplied to each, the information provider, the frequency of communication, the method of communication and the format. A pre-requisite for the communication plan is that all the external project stakeholders have been identified, a dialogue has been had with each to understand their information needs and any confidentiality requirements have been made explicit. Where possible, communication

---

4   World Bank stakeholder analysis guidelines can be found at: http://www1.worldbank.org/
     publicsector/anticorrupt/PoliticalEconomy/stakeholderanalysis.htm.

should be standardised, so that time-consuming bespoke reports do not have to be prepared for different stakeholders. This avoids the risk of the wrong information being issued to the wrong stakeholder.

CASE STUDY 6 – THE BIG DIG, USA

Boston's Central Artery/Tunnel Project (CA/T), commonly known as "The Big Dig", was the largest, most complex and technically challenging highway project in US history.[1] The main goals of the Big Dig project may be summarised as relieving highway traffic congestion, reducing bottlenecks in downtown Boston and decreasing the accident rate. The project had two main components: (1) replacing the six-lane elevated highway with an eight-to-10 lane underground expressway directly beneath the existing road, culminating at its northern limit into a 14-lane two-bridge crossing of the Charles River; and (2) the extension of I-90 (the Massachusetts Turnpike) from its former terminus south of downtown Boston through a tunnel beneath south Boston and Boston Harbour to Logan Airport. The project was originally scheduled to be completed in 1998, but was not finished until December 2007. Extensive environmental feasibility studies, risk assessments and other project activities were completed prior to the start of the project. However, costs increased across all contracts throughout the project's life cycle, despite enormous efforts to transfer, reduce or avoid adverse risks. In 1984, during the pre-development phase, the initial estimated cost to complete the Big Dig was approximately $2.3 billion. By 1989, project management estimated that construction would cost $4.4 billion, with estimated completion by 1998. On the completion of the project in 2007, the true cost of the project was estimated to be $14.625 billion, over six times that of the originally projected estimate.[2] It is thought that if there was a single cause of the very significant cost increase on the project, it was probably the project's complex procurement model.[3] The traditional design-bid-build model was adopted, resulting in the separate appointment of designers and contractors, which, it is claimed, provided little room for collaboration among the project's most important stakeholders.[4] Problems relating to project completion resulted in part from the sheer number of external stakeholders and the dynamic nature of their interaction. Each of the Big Dig's 110 major contracts involved intensely complicated technical, legal and economic issues. Planning for the project

---

1   massDOT (2013) "The Big Dig, Project Background", Massachusetts Department of Transportation, Highway Division, http:/www.massdot.state.ma.us/highway/TheBigDig/Project Background.aspx.
2   Zezima, K. (2004) "Big Dig Called Safe for Cars, But Not So for Pocketbooks", *New York Times*, 24 April, 26.
3   Greiman, V. (2012) "The Big Dig: Learning from a Mega Project", NASA Academy, http://www. nasa.gov/offices/oce/appel/ask/issues/39/39s_big_dig.html.
4   Ibid.

began in 1982, including stakeholder engagement with environmental agencies followed by environmental studies starting in 1983. The project received approval from the state environmental agencies in 1991 after satisfying various concerns, including the release of toxins by the excavation and the possibility of disrupting the homes of millions of rats.[5] By the time the federal environmental clearances were delivered in 1994, the process had taken some seven years, during which time inflation had increased the project's cost estimates considerably. In the early phases of the project, there was little communication between and among many of the external stakeholders. Community and social costs were vastly underestimated. Research suggests that no one on the project had envisioned the full cost of dealing with the media, community interests, numerous regulatory agencies, auditors and neighbourhood stakeholders. The unexpected discovery of 150-year-old revolutionary era sites and Native American artefacts resulted in the requirement for approval from yet another diverse set of stakeholders, including historical and preservation organisations and Native American groups. The key organisations involved in the Big Dig were as follows and in many cases the relationship between them was complex. The *Federal Highway Administration* (FHWA), an agency within the US Department of Transportation, provided oversight and management of federal project funds. (In accordance with the agreement signed with the Commonwealth of Massachusetts (CoM), the FHWA provided funding to the CA/T project through the Massachusetts Executive Office of Transportation and Construction (EOTC), which was acting on behalf of the Massachusetts Highway Department (MHD)). The *Massachusetts Turnpike Authority* (MTA) managed the project on behalf of the MHD through the use of an integrated project organisation (IPO), a joint venture of Bechtel Corporation and Parsons Brinkerhoff, Quade, and Douglas, Inc. The *Boston Transportation Planning Review* (BTPR) undertook the transportation planning program for metropolitan Boston during the early phases of the project. The EOTC fulfilled the role of a state department of transportation (DOT). *The Massachusetts Bay Transportation Authority* (MBTA) oversaw modes of transport other than roads. *Massport* was the organisation in control of the operation of airports and seaports within the state. Other parties involved but with a small role were as follows: the *Boston Redevelopment Authority* (BRA), the *Department of Public Works* and the *Massachusetts Department of Environmental Protection* (MassDEP). At different stages in the life of the project, several non-governmental organisations were involved in the consultation process, including the *Artery Business Committee*, the *Boston Chamber of Commerce*, which represented business community interests, and the *Boston Society of Landscape Architects*, a chapter of a national volunteer organisation for landscape professionals. Other organisations included in the process were concerned with the environment, such as the *Charles River Watershed Association* (CRWA) and the *Conservation Law Foundation*. Project opposition groups included *Citizens for a Livable Charlestown*, the *Sierra Club*

---

5   http:/en.wikipedia.org/wiki/Big_Dig.

and the *Committee for Regional Transportation*. The *North End Central Artery Advisory Committee*, a neighbourhood group, was specifically engaged in reviewing the alternative designs within the Greenway corridor.

External stakeholders are playing an ever-increasing role in the delivery of projects and while classification is helpful, there needs to be a realistic analysis of their impact to guide active management.

☑ Contractor participation in risk management is driven by contract obligations

Good contract risk management starts during the procurement phase with the development of appropriate risk management strategies.

State Government of Victoria,

Australia (Contract Management Guide)

When project sponsors and project managers seek to ensure specific contractor behaviour following the award of a contract, such as the management of uncertain events, it can only be guaranteed if the call for these behaviours is incorporated into the procurement process. Open and transparent contractor participation in PRM during project execution requires the tender and contract documents issued to stipulate the risk management activities that are to be performed. The contract clauses must be concise, unambiguous and prescriptive in terms of the risk process to be followed and the outputs required. The provision of the inclusion of risk management requirements may not be suitable for all contract types. This "rule" is based on the inclusion of risk management requirements within fixed-price lump-sum contracts (where it has already been extensively applied within the construction industry). A way of reinforcing the requirement for risk management is by stating that payment will be directly linked to the satisfactory completion of project delivery milestones or Key Performance Indicators (KPIs), where the means of achieving satisfactory outputs is clearly explained. The milestones must be realistic in terms of both their timeframe and the tasks to be completed (i.e. they can be undertaken by the contractor without having to rely on contributions from third parties outside of their control). Clearly, during the course of the works, a contractor is not going to share commercially sensitive information which would be detrimental to its interests. In addition, some contractors perceive the reporting of risks and issues as an opportunity to record where they are currently being or likely to be delayed by third parties, which does not represent the complete picture (the full risk exposure). This behaviour needs to be anticipated and challenged.

Risk management will provide a tool to use in the management of contractors in order to encourage them to be forward looking, to plan ahead, to test the robustness of their schedule and to consider those activities within the schedule which may be disrupted by adverse events. It will also support the drive to increase the float for particular activities within the schedule (to create a better buffer for protection against adverse events) and, if successfully protected, will present opportunities for exploitation leading to the potential for early completion. It also provides a tool to test expected productivity levels and hence satisfaction of the schedule. Productivity will be driven by the availability and management of the application of plant, labour and materials. Management activity is multi-faceted in that it must organise the use of labour whereby the correct quality is achieved, legislative requirements, drawings, specifications and local authority requirements (such as working hours, lorry movements and noise levels) are all adhered to and the schedule is maintained.

Contract clauses should be prepared to address the following topics:

1. *Risk representative*: a clause should call for the appointment of a risk representative within a fixed number of calendar days from the commencement of the contract. The contract can stipulate that that the representative will need to be approved by the client or his/her agents and that his/her CV will need to be submitted for review. In addition, the post holder will need to have had a specific number of years of experience of risk and project management, be conversant with international standard ISO 31000, be an effective facilitator and have strong written and oral communication skills. The risk representative will be required to prepare the risk management plan, arrange the risk management workshops, provide the risk reports, support the risk audits, maintain the risk records, complete the risk register (or database), provide internal risk management training and see that the risk management contract commitments are fulfilled.

2.   *Risk management plan*: a clause should call for the submission of a risk management plan within a fixed number of calendar days from the commencement of the contract. If a significant number of contracts are being awarded, it is often beneficial to issue the contractors with a risk management plan template for their adoption. Instructions can be given regarding the inclusion of their contract specific information within pre-determined locations in the plan. The issue of a template has a number of benefits. It speeds up the preparation of the plans and the commencement of risk management. It also ensures that the contractors use the same terms and definitions, risk management process (including the requirement to adopt ISO 31000), measures of probability and impact, stakeholder mapping, RACI[5] chart, workshop frequency and format, together with the same frequency and content of risk reports. The plan template can be used as a communication tool to capture and convey the project context, the project objectives, the role of the key parties, the risk management objectives and the building blocks for effective risk management.

3.   *Risk workshops*: a clause should call for the contractor to undertake regular risk workshops to identify the threats and potential opportunities (for exploitation) pertaining to his/her contract in order to ensure that the works are completed to the right quality, within the right timeframe and within the contract sum. It should be stipulated that the first workshop be held within a fixed number of calendar days from the commencement of the contract. The clause should stipulate the purpose and frequency of the workshops, who they should be chaired by, the competencies of the chairperson, the attendees, the required outputs and the application of the outputs. It should be stipulated that while threats and opportunities should be identified for the whole execution period, when a project spans many years, the contractor is to focus on events which may impact the next six months.

4.   *Risk register or risk database*: a clause should call for the submission of the first risk management register within a fixed number of calendar

---

5   RACI refers to a responsibility assignment matrix, which describes the participation of various roles in completing tasks or deliverables for a project. RACI is the acronym derived from the four key responsibilities most typically used: *Responsible, Accountable, Consulted and Informed*.

days from the commencement of the contract. If a significant number of contracts are being awarded, it is often beneficial to issue the contractors with a risk register template for their adoption so as to ensure that the submissions follow an identical format and contain at least the minimum information required. This will be particularly important if the intention is to carry out project-wide quantitative risk management. Where a project-wide risk database is being used to which the contractors will be afforded access, the contractors should be instructed as to the frequency of updating the database. In addition, the clause should state that access rights would be strictly controlled and that database training would be provided for those assigned access rights.

5. *Risk measurement*: risk measurement (such as probability impact grids) should be consistently applied to all contractors on a project so that the severity of risks can be compared across the different packages/contracts.

6. *Response planning*: emphasis should be placed on the need for response planning as opposed to merely capturing and reporting potential threats to the project's objectives. A clause should call for a specific focus on the identification and implementation of risk responses and the monitoring of their effectiveness. Each response should be unambiguous, concise, clearly understood and SMART (Specific, Measurable, Achievable, Relevant and Timebound). In other words, it should be:

    - specific in terms of seeking to reduce the probability of occurrence and/or impact of the threat;

    - measurable in terms of being able to readily discern if the response has been completed or not;

    - achievable in the sense that the response can be implemented by the risk actionee (the individual assigned with the responsibility for implementing the response) without involving third parties;

    - relevant in that the response(s) will address the threat being addressed; and

•   timebound whereby the response(s) will be implemented sufficiently in advance of the date when it is anticipated that the threat will materialise so as to ensure that the project schedule will remain unaffected.

7.   *Risk reporting*: a contract clause should call for the reports to be supplied, the information they should contain and the timing of their submission. In addition, if it is required that summary information should be included in dashboards or monthly progress presentations, then this stipulation should be described in detail, for instance, the number of risks to be included in the dashboard and the accompanying risk information to be captured.

8.   *Risk audit*: a contract clause should stipulate that the contractor's risk management practices would be subject to regular audits (such as every six months) in order to ensure their compliance with the contract and their risk management plan.

> Clear unequivocal clauses need to be included in traditional construction contracts if contractors are to be able to price for and implement PRM in a way that the project considers will contribute to effective risk management.

4

Organisation

☑ **Risk management aspirations need to be rooted in reality**

The risk management capabilities of an organisation will be highly dependent on the level of risk management maturity the organisation has reached.

Robert Chapman, author

Projects wishing to implement risk management need to understand that the realisation of effective risk management will not be instant. It is most probable that highly developed risk management practices will not be possible "out of the starting blocks" or be capable of being established "overnight". The level of risk management maturity assumed to be attainable by consultancies (that have secured a commission against a financial and technical bid) and are already committed (by way of their bid) to a scope and method of implementation of risk management, may be a fallacy. In addition, organisations that regularly undertake projects "in-house" and have well-developed risk processes may still falter in developing mature practices due to, for instance, team formation,culture, budget or decision-making issues. Mature PRM practices typically take time to develop. There will be a myriad of factors which will need to be addressed to achieve risk management practices which enhance project performance. Some of these factors are examined in turn below:

- *Project leadership*: from experience, a high proportion of project staff in senior management positions do not possess project management or risk management qualifications or have had no formal risk management training. The experience of the senior management team will be significant in affecting their adopted approach to risk management (commonly referred to as the "tone at the top") and be very influential in "colouring" the risk management culture.[1]

---

1 For further guidance on risk culture, see the Institute of Risk Management's publications "Risk Culture: Under the Microscope, Guidance for Boards" and "Risk Culture, Resources for

- *Risk budget*: significantly, in many cases, those who prepared the budget for staff resource levels for a project will not be the same individuals that will implementing it. In addition, the "authors" of the budget may not have consulted a risk practitioner when determining the level and length of involvement. As such, there may be a mismatch between the deliverables and the budget. If it is insufficient, the budget will be one of the largest constraints on the development of risk management practices from the outset.

- *Experience of working together*: given the advances in technology (leading to an ever-increasing number of discipline specialists), organisation staff turnover rates and the common practice of creating a new team for each project, it is highly probable that many of the team members will never have worked together before. This is more prevalent in large-scale infrastructure projects around the world, where teams are largely assembled from multinational expatriates. This is significant as they will most likely be used to working in different ways.

- *Experience of risk management*: among team members there will be differences in terms of the level of risk management training, competence, awareness and predisposition. Each team member is likely to have a different experience of the application of risk management (if any at all) and a different opinion as to its "value-add" and how it should be implemented. In addition, each will have worked to different risk management plans and scoring schemes.

- *Participation in risk management*: when project disciplines establish their resource levels to implement a project, they invariably do not factor in the time they will need to spend with other disciplines and project management functions. Specifically, time is not allocated for attending risk workshops, risk meetings, adopting a risk-based approach to option analysis, populating spreadsheets or a risk database, contributing to risk reports or making presentations to the client/sponsor on risk response plans for the risks for which they are the named actionee.

Practitioners" published in 2012. See also the Institute of Risk Management's "Risk Appetite and Risk Tolerance", published in 2011.

- *Project failures*: team members will have had different experiences of project failure as well as varying degrees of appreciation of their causes and how failure might have been prevented by the application of risk management practices. Common problems centre on the inappropriate selection of contracts, contractors, the number of contract packages and the degree of risk transfer, all of which can be evaluated with the aid of risk management processes.

- *Terms and definitions*: at the outset in all probability, team members will have a different understanding of the common terms of risk management. In addition, there may be strongly held opinions, leading to a lack of agreement on the definition of specific terms. This may sound trivial, but a lack of an agreed common language can lead to immediate difficulties.

- *Incorporation*: those who have not adopted risk management for business case assessment, gate reviews, option analysis, feasibility studies or the evaluation of alternative procurement routes will not automatically think to apply the discipline of risk management at these times. The ease of inculcating risk management will be directly proportionate to former practices.

The Current Level of Risk Management Maturity

As a result of these factors and many others, a plan will need to be developed for the progressive development and integration of risk management practices. The status of risk management at the outset of a project will need to be reflected in the project and organisation objectives for risk management. The old adage "you need to be able to walk before you can run" is just as applicable to PRM. Projects that attempt to rush headlong into sophisticated risk management processes without benchmarking current competencies will most likely run into difficulties very quickly. Hence, before risk management frameworks, policies, plans and procedures are prepared, there needs to be an assessment of the current and desired level of risk maturity of the organisation and the project. A suitable tool to benchmark risk maturity is a "risk maturity model" (RMM).

The Concept of Maturity Models

The concept of maturity models to measure capabilities is well developed and accepted. The development of RMMs stems primarily from the Capability Maturity Model (CMM) developed at the Software Engineering Institute (SEI)[2] located at Carnegie Mellon University in Pittsburgh, Pennsylvania. An RMM provides a means of identifying the current level of risk management capability of a project or organisation and is a tool to support a structured approach to process improvement. RMMs are constructed as matrices based on three components, namely levels of maturity, assessment perspectives and competencies (practices or attributes) within each perspective, as illustrated in Figure 4.1 below. Five levels and four perspectives are included in the figure, but this is for illustrative purposes only, the actual number being at the discretion of the author of the model. The arrow merely indicates the direction of increasing maturity.

Risk Maturity Model				
	Perspective 1	Perspective 2	Perspective 3	Perspective 4
Level 5	Competencies	Competencies	Competencies	Competencies
Level 4	Competencies	Competencies	Competencies	Competencies
Level 3	Competencies	Competencies	Competencies	Competencies
Level 2	Competencies	Competencies	Competencies	Competencies
Level 1	Competencies	Competencies	Competencies	Competencies

Figure 4.1   Components of a maturity model

Hence, in general terms, an RMM is a representation of a small number of incremental ascending levels of risk maturity to enable organisations to appraise their risk management competency and plan improvements which

---

2   The Software Engineering Institute (SEI) is a federally funded research and development centre sponsored by the US Department of Defense. It has been developing its CMM since 1998. The conceptual framework for the CMM was developed by Watts Humphrey.

will permit a progressive drive towards greater benefits. RMMs can be used in a structured process to understand current risk management competencies, where and how improvement may be achieved, and establish long-term goals for enhancing maturity. An example of an RMM developed to understand strengths and weaknesses in risk management is the US cybersecurity RMM described in Case Study 7. It is aimed at improving the security of the US energy infrastructure and ensuring that the country's electrical systems remain secure, reliable and resilient. RMMs are a natural starting point for organisations wishing to inculcate risk management as a project discipline. They can be used to answer the questions of "what is it we want to accomplish with risk management?" and "what resources will it take to realise those benefits?". On the basis that organisations and projects are unable to make a single jump from unsophisticated to highly developed, incremental steps need to be defined.

The Value of RMMs

The value of RMMs will depend on their composition and application. Each level needs to be readily distinguishable from its neighbour and a logical progression needs to be created between successive levels. Each level and perspective needs to be identified by a concise descriptor. In particular, the perspectives need to be selected from a combination of proven organisational analysis focus areas (such as those described in the European Foundation for Quality Management (EFQM) Excellence Model) and PRM practices (such as those described in the Association for Project Management PRAM Guide). In addition, the perspectives combined with the competencies (described within each perspective) need to be suitable to measure effective risk management. A key question is whether the achievement of the competencies described will lead to an optimisation of processes and capabilities, and the elimination of deficient practices. A weakness of early RMMs is that the selection of perspectives was not explained, they were not accompanied by a descriptor and they did not address all areas that could affect effective risk management.

Existing Risk Maturity Models

There are a number of approaches to benchmarking relevant to implementing risk management. These include the Central Computer and

Telecommunications Agency (CCTA),[3] Hillson,[4] DeLoach,[5] Chapman,[6] PMI,[7] OGC,[8, 9] Deloitte,[10] Hopkinson[11] and Antonucci.[12] This is not an exhaustive list and the DeLoach, Chapman and Deloitte approaches are tailored to enterprise risk management. The first approach listed was published by the CCTA in 1993, which was composed of four levels of risk maturity (as described in Appendix H) and was succeeded by the now more well-known Hillson RMM. Hillson proposes an RMM and describes guidance to organisations wishing to develop or improve their approach to risk management, allowing them to assess their current level of maturity, identify realistic targets for improvement and develop action plans for increasing their risk capability. The Hillson model (see Appendix H) is composed of four levels, which are described in ascending order as "naive", "novice", "normalised" and "natural". The four levels are illustrated in Figure 4.2 below.

It is not known how this choice of labels has been received in practice, particularly when current competencies are described as "naive", for instance. Hillson recognises that some organisations may not fit neatly into these capability levels, but considers the RMM levels to be sufficiently different to accommodate most organisations unambiguously, considering that more than four levels would increase ambiguity without giving sufficient additional refinement to aid the use of the model.

---

3   CCTA (1993) "Introduction to the Management of Risk" published by the Government Centre for Information Systems in October 1993 and authored by Scarff, Carty and Charette.

4   Hillson, D. (1997) "Towards a Risk Maturity Model", *International Journal of Project and Business Risk Management*, 1(1), 34–45.

5   DeLoach, J.W. (2000) *Enterprise-Wide Risk Management: Strategies for Linking Risk with Opportunity*. London: Financial Times/Prentice Hall.

6   Chapman, R.J. (2006) *Simple Tools and Techniques for Enterprise Risk Management*. Chichester: John Wiley & Sons.

7   PMI (2008) *Organisational Project Management Maturity Model (OPM3®) Knowledge Foundation*, 2nd edn. Newtown Square, PA: Project Management Institute Inc.

8   OGC (2007) *Management of Risk: Guidance for Practitioners*. London: The Stationery Office.

9   OGC (2010) *Portfolio, Programme and Project Management Maturity Model (P3M3®), Introduction and Guide to P3M3®*, Version 2.1. Crown Copyright.

10 Deloitte Touche Tohmatsu (2008) "Designing a Successful ERM Function: A Global Perspective on Risk Management Structure and Governance for the Insurance Industry".

11 Hopkinson, M. (2011) *The Project Risk Maturity Model: Measuring and Improving Risk Management Capability*. Farnham: Gower Publishing.

12 Domenic Antonucci is the Chief Risk Officer at ADPC Abu Dhabi Ports Co., UAE, who presented his "Risk Maturity Model dedicated to ISO 31000" at the first ISO 31000 Risk Management Conference in Paris on 21 and 22 May 2012. See his session here: http://conference2012.g31000.org/day-2.html.

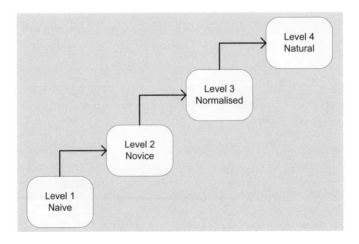

Figure 4.2   The four levels of the Hillson risk maturity model

The Hopkinson Model

The most comprehensive approach to both describing a RMM and its implementation is that proposed by Hopkinson.[13] Hopkinson acknowledges that his RMM is directly derived from the structure developed by Hillson described above. Progress up the risk management levels is not commonly achieved simultaneously across all perspectives. Hopkinson makes the important statement that the overall risk management capability of a project is only equal to the weakest capability among his six perspectives. The justification is that process capability for each perspective is critical to the effectiveness of the overall risk management process. He makes the salient point that "there is little point in having state of the art risk analysis, if the risk identification processes are so ineffective that many of the important risks are ignored".[14] For those contemplating constructing their own maturity model, the Hopkinson RMM may be a good starting point. However, before adopting this model as a foundation, certain aspects of its construction warrant closer scrutiny. The first observation is there is no debate about the appropriate number of maturity levels. Second, the level descriptions are very brief and are not very informative. Third, there is no explanation of how the six perspectives were arrived at. Fourth, the 50 project RMM questions are not described in a single location, which hinders the ability to quickly assimilate their coverage.

---

13 See note 11 above.
14 Hopkinson, M. (2000) "Risk Maturity Models in Practice", *Risk Management Bulletin*, 5(4), 25–9.

Fifth, the 50 questions do not address, for instance, a risk framework, the project context or integration with all of the leading project management disciplines.

CASE STUDY 7 – ELECTRIC SECTOR CYBERSECURITY RISK MATURITY PROJECT, USA

A US Department of Energy (DOE) initiative (supported by an advisory group, a model development team, subject-matter experts and a model architect from the Carnegie Mellon University Software Engineering Institute – CERT Program) has produced a cybersecurity RMM for the energy subsector. At the time of the announcement of the initiative, White House Cybersecurity Coordinator Howard Schmidt said: "it is important to understand the sector's strengths and remaining gaps across the grid to inform investment planning and research and development and enhance our public-private partnership efforts". The model was developed in support of the "Electricity Subsector Cybersecurity Risk Management Maturity Initiative", a White House initiative led by the DOE in partnership with the Department of Homeland Security (DHS) and in collaboration with representatives of asset owners and operators within the electricity subsector. On the launch of the project, US Energy Secretary Steven Chu said: "this initiative is another important step in improving the security of the nation's energy infrastructure and ensuring that the country's electrical systems remain secure, reliable and resilient". The electricity portion of the energy sector includes the generation, transmission, distribution and marketing of electricity. The use of electricity is ubiquitous, spanning all sectors of the US economy. The electric power subsector accounts for 40 per cent of all energy consumed in the US. Electricity system facilities are dispersed throughout the North American continent. The model was developed to apply to all electric utilities, regardless of ownership structure, size or function. Broad use of the model is expected to support benchmarking for the subsector's cybersecurity capabilities. The goal of the model is to support ongoing development and measurement of cybersecurity capabilities within the electricity subsector through the following four objectives: [1] strengthening cybersecurity capabilities in the electricity subsector; [2] enabling utilities to effectively and consistently evaluate and benchmark cybersecurity capabilities, [3] share knowledge, best practices and relevant references within the subsector as a means improving cybersecurity capabilities; and [4] enabling utilities to prioritise actions and investments to improve cybersecurity. This initial version of the model was developed from January to May 2012. The model is arranged as a matrix and is organised into 10 domains (columns) and four maturity indicator level (MIL) rows. At the intersection of each domain and MIL, there is a set of practices that defines the domain for that MIL. Each domain is a logical grouping of cybersecurity practices. A domain's practices are organised by MIL to define the progression of maturity for the domain. The model's construction is described in Appendix K.

Rate of Improvement

Organisations implementing projects need to recognise that performance improvement in risk management (guided by a maturity model) needs to be seen as a long-term process, as illustrated in Figure 4.3 below. Effective and enduring changes in culture, procedures and processes to support risk management can take many months (or in some cases years) to implement. When the next level is reached, time is needed to ensure that the level is established and maintained, and the practices described within it become ingrained in the organisation. In addition, there should be recognition that the highest level of maturity (depending on its composition) may never be reached.

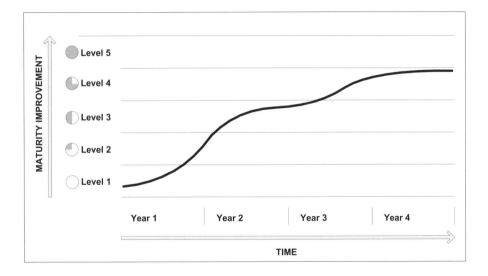

Figure 4.3   Performance improvement is time-dependent

Building a Risk Maturity Model

The important point about RMMs is that "one size does not fit all". This is illustrated by Case Study 7, where considerable time, effort and energy were invested in developing a bespoke RMM to suit a specific set of circumstances (recognising in this instance that it was a rather special case). Another aspect of an RMM is that it is a communication tool, so it must be accompanied with an explanation of "why is it advantageous?". There needs to be an explanation as to why it is important that the project or organisation gains these maturity levels. The model itself and this explanation need to be developed with senior management so that there is ownership of the desire to implement change "at the top". When tailoring an existing RMM or building one from scratch, careful thought needs to be given to current risk management capabilities (the starting point), realistic goals (the ultimate maturity level) and the need to be able to communicate intermediate improvements (interim levels). Implementing an RMM should be thought of as implementing a schedule or programme of activities whereby when all of the activities have been successfully completed, the risk management objectives have been satisfied. The lowest level of maturity should reflect the current position rather than a maturity level already passed or one that it is hoped will be reached. The highest level of maturity selected should in part reflect the amount of time available to implement improvements. For instance, a single project in most cases will not provide the opportunity to make significant improvements, whereas a department continuously implementing a number of projects over many years will most likely permit the realisation of several levels of improvement. Prior to constructing an RMM, a rigorous examination of the PLC should be undertaken, examining the risk management practices that will be employed at each stage (and the gates in between if appropriate). This will inform the levels, perspectives and competencies required. Each perspective (as described above) must be a logical grouping of competencies. The perspectives should address all of the risk management process steps and how risk management will be integrated into the project(s). Hence, the perspectives should address such subjects as the development of the risk framework, policy, plan and process, lessons learned, stakeholder management, integration with other project disciplines and project management activities (such as the development of the gate process, the business case, the execution plan, the project brief and the project controls).

Use of a Risk Maturity Model

An RMM can be used as a road map to describe "where you are" and "where you want to get to". However, an RMM is only a statement of intent and does not become reality without implementation. A plan needs to be established with the goal of attaining the desired level of maturity. This plan is likely to be based on incremental improvements, such as using the RMM levels as stepping stones rather than striving to gain all desired improvements in a single step. The plan should be supported by a schedule (created with the aid of a suitable planning software tool) that captures all of the competencies to be achieved, the activities to be undertaken to accomplish them and their respective durations. Progress in implementing the activities can then be readily monitored. The schedule may be resource loaded, so responsibility for undertaking the activities can be recorded to support implementation. When obstacles are met and activities take longer to implement than anticipated, as will almost certainly be the case, the schedule should be updated accordingly. An independent third party should be engaged to assess on a periodic basis the level of maturity reached and the drawbacks to the project arising from the lack of achievement of specific competencies.

At the outset, when risk management is first contemplated, there needs to be a conservation based on a number of questions, such as: what is the aim of implementing risk management? Are our aims realistic? What is the current level of risk management maturity? Will risk management need to be implemented in stages? What time do we have available? What is a realistic maturity target?

☑ The risk profile of a project will be directly influenced by the procurement process

> *The involvement of multiple parties in a project introduces uncertainty about important issues that can give rise to massive uncertainty with significant risk and opportunity implications.*
>
> Chapman, C. and Ward, S. (2011)
> How to Manage Project Opportunity and Risk:
> Why Uncertainty Management Can Be a Much Better Approach than
> Risk Management, *3rd edn. Chichester: John Wiley & Sons.*

The vast majority of projects are not executed by a single organisation, but involve the appointment of a contractor (or contractors) and suppliers to carry out the works. The typical procurement process will entail making a significant number of decisions, all of which have attendant risks. Some of the common decisions to be made are included in Appendix J. Perhaps the five most important decisions are the selection of: the project scope (scale of project), the procurement method, the tender and award process, the contract conditions and the contractor.

Determination of the Project Scope/Scale

The project scope requires careful consideration from a number of perspectives. Has the organisation sufficient funds for the scope envisaged? Will funding be derived from capital already held by the business or will the business need to borrow? The scale of the borrowings, the payback period and the interest payments could affect the business as a whole, not just the project. If the project is modernising, extending or re-equipping existing premises, the scale of the project requires consideration in terms of disruption to ongoing activities. For very large projects, as part of the business case, consideration needs to be given to market capacity, contractor capabilities and the practicalities of implementation. Clearly project execution can be subdivided between a number of contractors, but this then introduces the dimension of interface management. In these circumstances, there needs to be clear recognition of the need for and assignment of responsibility for managing the interfaces between the contracting parties. If an organisation overreaches itself with an overambitious project, what are the ramifications of this? An example of a project where the scale and complexity were misjudged (as identified by the National Audit Office) is the National Programme for IT within the NHS given in Case Study 8.

CASE STUDY 8 – THE NATIONAL PROGRAMME FOR IT IN THE NHS, UK

In a press release issued by the National Audit Office in May 2011, its head, Amyas Morse, stated: "The original vision for the National Programme for IT in the NHS will not be realised. The NHS is now getting far fewer systems than planned despite the Department paying contractors almost the same amount of money. This is yet another example of a department fundamentally underestimating the scale and complexity of a major IT-enabled change programme."

The original central aim of the Programme was the creation of a fully integrated electronic care records system designed to reduce reliance on paper files, make accurate patient records available at all times and enable the rapid transmission of information between different parts of the NHS. The system was intended to include a Detailed Care Record and a Summary Care Record for each NHS patient. The press release stated: "The rate at which electronic care records systems are being put in place across the NHS under the National Programme for IT is falling far below expectations and the core aim that every patient should have an electronic care record under the Programme will not now be achieved. Even where systems have been delivered, they are not yet able to do everything that the Department intended, especially in acute trusts. Moreover, the number of systems to be delivered through the Programme has been significantly reduced, without a commensurate reduction in the cost." The press release went on to say that: "Today's NAO report[1] concludes that the £2.7 billion spent so far on care records systems does not represent value for money. And, based on performance so far, the NAO has no grounds for confidence that the remaining planned spending of £4.3 billion on care records systems will be any different." The Health Secretary Andrew Lansley, the Cabinet Office Minister Francis Maude and NHS chief executive Sir David Nicholson decided that it was better to discontinue the programme rather than put even more money into it.

---

1   NAO (2011) "The National Programme for IT in the NHS: An Update on the Delivery of Detailed Care Records Systems", Report by the Comptroller and Auditor General, 18 May.

Choice of Procurement Method for Construction Projects

The ability to manage risk on a project where more than one party is responsible for its execution will be dictated by the "procurement method" selected. The term "procurement method" is used to describe the complex arrangement of relationships which are formed between the client, the consultants and the delivery companies. For construction projects, the selection of the procurement method will be influenced by a client's prioritised objectives, which typically include cost, time and quality. The procurement method and the specific contract selected to satisfy these prioritised objectives will incorporate an allocation of responsibility between the parties for managing project uncertainty. From a client's perspective, this allocation will influence how uncertainty is managed and whether it will be managed in his best or her interests. Clearly, the two parties will have different abilities and motivations for managing risk. Both parties will be seeking to enhance their bottom line performance and hence the client will seek to minimise his or her costs and the contractor will seek to maximise his or her profits. To this end, the client will seek to minimise uncertainty and wherever possible the contractor will commonly seek to exploit uncertainty.

Procurement Methods

It is generally accepted that there are three key methods of procurement, namely the traditional or conventional approach, design and build, and management. Over and above these three are several variations increasing the number of available methods. Which procurement method is likely to be the most appropriate in any given situation will depend on the scope of work, the complexity of the design, where the responsibility for design is to be placed, how the work is to be coordinated, on what price basis the contract is to be awarded, how quickly the project is to be completed, what level of finish is required and how the risks are to be allocated or shared between the contract parties. Each procurement type has a different risk transfer (i.e. sharing) profile in terms of the degree to which risk is transferred to the contractor or retained by the client (see Figure 4.4). Usually risk is only retained by the client if there is an advantage in doing so. If for instance a computer microchip production facility is only viable if it can be produced within a particular timeframe then using the management contracting method (for instance) may be appropriate.

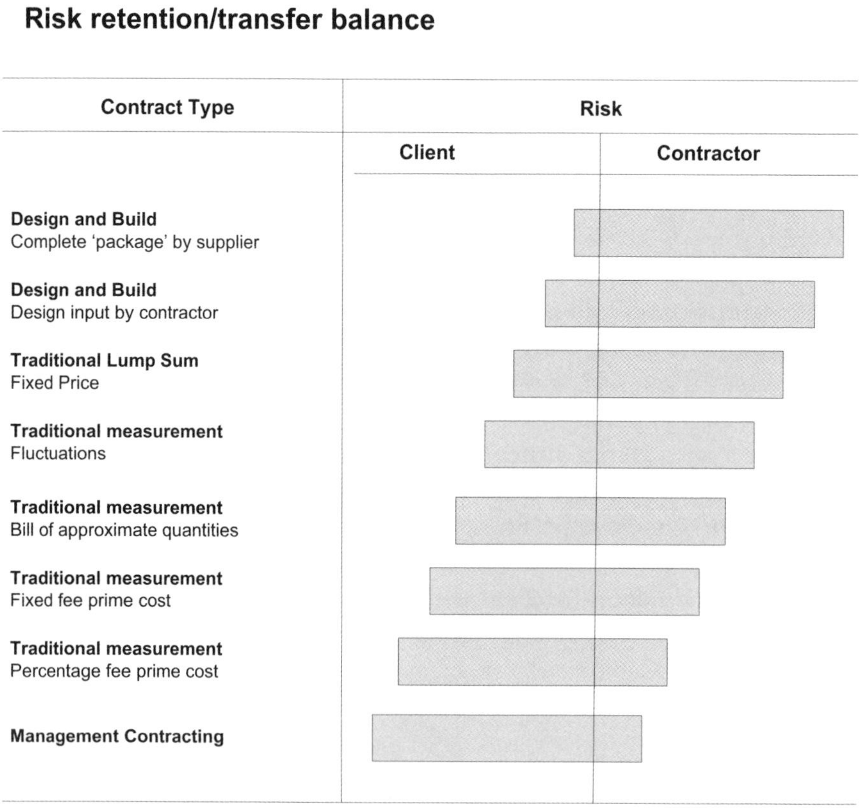

Risk retention/transfer balance

Contract Type	Risk	
	Client	Contractor
Design and Build Complete 'package' by supplier		
Design and Build Design input by contractor		
Traditional Lump Sum Fixed Price		
Traditional measurement Fluctuations		
Traditional measurement Bill of approximate quantities		
Traditional measurement Fixed fee prime cost		
Traditional measurement Percentage fee prime cost		
Management Contracting		

Figure 4.4   Degree of risk transfer to the contractor with different procurement methods

Source: Lupton, S. (2007) *Which Contract? Choosing the Appropriate Building Contract*, 4th edn. London: RIBA Publishing)

Procurement Using Traditional Methods

The traditional lump-sum (fixed-price) method typically entails the client appointing design, cost control and project management consultants, and a main contractor who is responsible for completing the work. This method is based on the design being completed prior to the commencement of the work. The contractor is responsible for the procurement of plant, labour and materials, together with supplier and subcontractor performance. The contractor is normally chosen after competitive tendering on documents that describe the full extent of the work (or defining where specific aspects are covered by provisional sums). However, the contractor can be appointed either through negotiation or on the basis of partial or notional information. This approach requires a full set of documents before tenders are invited. This method provides certainty of cost, to the extent that a price is agreed before commencement. However, it cannot guarantee a specified outturn cost as it will not be able to remove all the sources of uncertainty. In addition, while competitive tendering adopting this method is perceived as an efficient way of obtaining value for money, it is dependent on the client being aware of the project costs and the contractor's level of profit. This is because with a lump-sum contract, the client pays the price to the contractor regardless of what the contract actually costs the contractor to complete the works. Under this type of contract, the contractor is motivated to reduce his or her costs while at the same time (it is hoped) not prejudicing the quality of the completed works. In times of a weak economy and infrequent contracts, the contractor who deliberately (or accidentally) underestimates the risks will most likely win the tender. Under these circumstances, in the event of risks materialising which the contractor is expected to absorb, the contractor will seek an increase in his or her price and/or instigate a claims process to address his or her losses.

A now well-known London landmark is the Shard (described in Case Study 9), where the final contract form chosen was a fixed-price contract to provide greater cost certainty.

CASE STUDY 9 – THE SHARD, LONDON, UK

The Shard, which has received considerable media attention, is located on the south bank of the Thames in London. At 310 metres (1,017 feet) in height, it is the tallest building in Western Europe. The building takes its name from the concept architect Renzo Piano, who described the project "as a shard of glass" during the planning stages. The 72 habitable floors comprise a mix of 600,000 square feet of office space, three floors of restaurants, 10 residences, a number of retail units, a 200-bed hotel and a public viewing gallery. The building was described by Piano as "a vertical city with many functions". The construction began in March 2009 and the external envelope was completed in 2012. Originally the building was planned to be executed as a construction management contract, but prior to the commencement of the works, the procurement strategy "morphed" to a negotiated Joint Contracts Tribunal (JCT) fixed-price contract. As a consequence, price risk was passed on to the contractor. However, at the time of the change in contract, the value of the packages already let represented some 70 per cent of the project value. Hence, the degree of risk exposure for the contractor was significantly less than it might have been. The programme duration of 38 weeks, necessitating the construction of a floor every seven days, represented a major risk for the contractor. The completion date was under pressure from the required pace of construction combined with the restricted site, very tight building frame tolerances, the proximity of the basement to London Bridge railway station, the requirement for novel construction practices, lack of space for site storage and high winds. This case study is of note in that the client became more risk averse (financially) through seeking a contract that afforded greater price certainty and additionally elected for a tried-and-tested form of contract which is readily understood in the construction industry.

Procurement Using Design and Build Methods

The contractor is responsible for all or part of the design as well as carrying out the works. The arrangement may be for total design and build or for design development post-completion of the scheme design prepared and supplied by the client's consultants. The contractor will appoint his or her own design consultants to complete the element of design for which he or she is responsible. The contractor may be appointed by competitive tender or as a result of a negotiated agreement. Frequently with this procurement method, the client will seek for the contractor to appoint one, some or all of his or her own consultants at the time the design and build contract is entered into. This process is usually referred to as consultant switch or novation. The benefit of this method is that it avoids exposing the client to disputes between the contractor and one or more of the designers in terms of the timing, completeness, accuracy or coordination of the design. The client will lack control over the detailed aspects of the design; however, this may be acceptable for simple buildings such as industrial buildings. Construction work can start earlier than the traditional method as construction and design can be overlapped to a degree.

Procurement Using Management Methods

There are two main forms of management procurement in the UK: *management contracts* and *construction management* contracts.

With *management* contracts, the client typically starts by appointing a project manager and design consultants to prepare project drawings and a project specification. The management contractor is selected by a process of tender and interviews and is paid on the basis of scheduled services, prime costs and management fees. This contractor's primary role is to manage the execution of the work. Commonly, he or she is not directly involved in carrying out any of the construction work. This is carried out as individual packages by works contractors usually appointed by the management contractor. Hence, the works contractors are directly and contractually responsible to the management contractor. This approach has the ability to overlap design and construction and commence construction before all of the design is complete. It has the flexibility to change the sequence of packages and amend the extent of design and construction overlap as work progresses.

With *construction management* contracts, there is usually a lead designer responsible for overall design and a construction manager responsible for the management and coordination of work, with the client responsible for directing the project and entering into all of the works contracts directly. Construction management offers the advantage of speed, but not price certainty, as the true cost of the project is not known until the last contract has been let.

Effective risk analysis and management is fundamental to all forms of project procurement, including construction management. But construction management places a higher risk with the client than other forms of procurement because there is no main contractor. This suggests that under construction management, the client should place a greater premium on risk management than with other approaches. However, as outlined in the description of the Holyrood Project (see Case Study 10), the client's comprehension of the procurement method chosen and the inherent apportionment of risk was clearly lacking.

CASE STUDY 10 – THE HOLYROOD PROJECT, SCOTLAND[1]

The Scottish Parliament Building (known as the Holyrood Project) was initiated in 1997 and was opened in 2004. In general, each procurement route has its own advantages and disadvantages and selection must be based on the client's objectives. However, the project did not prepare a comprehensive procurement strategy document which would have included a reasoned analysis of the different procurement options, to what degree each one satisfied the project objectives, the risk associated with each and a strategy to manage those risks which would be retained by the client. The procurement method selected was construction management; however, the client had no experience of this particular method. Due to significant delays and increasing costs, the Auditor General for Scotland was called upon to examine and report on the project, in which he stated that: "The difficulties of delivering the Holyrood building using the 'construction management' method of procurement lie at the heart of the problems that arose."[2] In the Auditor's report, he drew attention to the fact that with this method, most of the risks stay with the client rather than transferring to the contractors. He remarked: "There should have been a systematic assessment of the risks implicit in the chosen procurement route (designer appointment and subsequent construction management) and how best to manage those risks." Lord Fraser remarked in the Holyrood Inquiry Report that: "It verges on the embarrassing to conclude, as I do, that virtually none of the key questions about construction management were asked. Similarly none of the disadvantages of construction management appear to have been identified and evaluated." He went on to say that "the selection of Construction Management was the single factor to which most of the misfortunes that have befallen the Project can be attributed."[3] In his 2000 report, the Auditor General stated that "there should have been an analysis of how to use incentive structures to promote added value in the design and construction processes. A common practice in major construction projects, where deadlines are tight, is to seek to ensure that contractors meet the required performance level through financial bonuses for early completion and penalties for delays. As the history of the project shows … there were significant risks to the overall cost and programme during the design phase, and those risks crystallised".[4] The prime reason for the project delays was the late issue of design information (arising from extensive design development). These delays led to contractor claims for prolongation, delay and disruption.

---

1   Auditor General (2004) "Management of the Holyrood building project" prepared by the Auditor General for Scotland, licensed under the Open Government Licence
2   Auditor General for Scotland (2004) "Management of the Holyrood Building Project".
3   (2004) "The Holyrood Inquiry, A Report by the Rt Hon Lord Fraser of Carmyllie QC on His Inquiry into the Holyrood Building Project", Clerk of the Scottish Parliament, 15 September.
4   Auditor General for Scotland and Audit Scotland (2000) "The New Scottish Parliament Building: An Examination of the Management of the Holyrood Project", September.

At the time of the 2004 audit, the estimated final cost of 41 of the 58 individual trade contracts was 21 per cent or more above the cost plan allowance. These contracts accounted for 91 per cent of the estimated contract expenditure. The estimated cost increased by some £220 million and there was a slippage of 20 months over a period of four years.

The Tender and Award Process

The tender process above all else should be fair and transparent and organisations and government departments must follow and be seen to follow their own published procedures and regulations. An example of a risk materialising where a government department did not follow the procurement regulations leading to legal action by an unsuccessful tenderer is described in Case Study 11 below.

Invitation to Tender

The tender period provided to tenderers needs to be adequate for the scale, complexity and geographical reach of the project (as in transport projects). When a programme for award slips, clients frequently reduce the tender period to make up time. This could lead to a number of scenarios. Tenders may decline to tender, ask for longer to tender, submit a tender on time but increase the sum added for risk or make mistakes. None of these scenarios is beneficial to the client. The golden rules of tender documentation are clarity, consistency and completeness. The tenderers will have limited time to carry out a considerable amount of work and the party issuing the documents should ensure that they are readily understood.

Award Criteria

Commonly the award criteria are extensive and include, for instance, team working arrangements, proposals for managing the contract (such as safety, quality, environmental, execution and risk plans and programming including milestones), project team organisation, technical suitability (including experience) and services provided by others.

Weighting of Award Criteria

Tenderers should be assessed on how well they satisfy the award criteria. The relative importance of each criterion should be established by giving it a percentage weighting so that all the weightings equal 100 per cent. It is common that a weighting is applied to the technical and price submissions, so, for instance, a weighting of 60 per cent may be applied to technical submissions and 40 per cent to price submissions where the technical quality of a bid is seen as the priority.

CASE STUDY 11 – PORTCULLIS HOUSE, LONDON, UK

Portcullis House, funded by the UK government and overseen by officials of the House of Commons, was completed in August 2000. The building, located in Westminster, provides offices for 210 Members of Parliament (MPs) and 400 staff, together with Select Committee and meeting rooms, a restaurant and a cafeteria. It largely completes a long-standing programme to increase the accommodation for MPs and others working in the Palace of Westminster, and to provide an office for every MPs who wants one. All the main construction contracts were let after competitive tendering. However, the House incurred legal and settlement costs totalling some £9.9 million after it was successfully sued by an unsuccessful tenderer for unfair treatment and contravention of procurement regulations in relation to the cladding and fenestration contract (pre-fabricated wall and window units). The unsuccessful tenderer's price was £2 million cheaper than that of the successful tenderer.

Contract Conditions

Contract conditions will protect a project owner from risk exposure if adequately defined and implemented. Surety bonds are increasingly popular with owners to protect their interests. The idea behind a surety bond is straightforward. One organisation guarantees to another that a third organisation will perform. In contract language, a surety bond is a written agreement whereby one party, called the *surety*, obliges itself to a second party, called the *obligee*, to answer for the default of a third party, called the principal or *obligor*. Surety bonds in construction contracts are called *contract surety bonds*. There are three types of contract surety bonds: *bid bonds*, *performance bonds* and *payment bonds*:

- A *bid bond* is a promise from a surety for a construction contract to guarantee that the bidder, if awarded the contract within the time stipulated, will enter into the contract at the price bid and will furnish the prescribed performance bond. Default ordinarily will result in the liability of the obligee for the difference between the amount of the principal's bid and the bid of the next lowest bidder who can qualify for the contract.

- A *performance bond* is a promise from the bonding company ("the surety") to perform those obligations in an amount up to but not exceeding the amount of the bond. A performance bond protects the owner from financial loss should the contractor fail to perform the contract in accordance with its terms and conditions.

- A *payment bond* is a promise from a surety that guarantees payment to certain subcontractors, labourers and suppliers for the labour and materials used in the work performed under the contract. These bonds protect labourers and suppliers in the event that the contractor fails to pay them.

To protect project owners against late delivery, liquidated damages (LDs) may be imposed. LDs are a specific sum of money stipulated by the contracting parties as the amount to be recovered for each day of delay in delivery of the product or completion of the contract. They do not present actual damages, but are established in the initial contract as a substitute for actual damages. They should represent as far as possible the most realistic forecast of what the actual damages are likely to be. Contractor liability under LDs is almost always capped at some percentage of the construction cost.

Other contract conditions (too numerous to describe here) may address intellectual property rights, copyright, contacting the media, milestones, completion date, design warranties, material and workmanship warranties, default and termination.

Remedies to Address Poor Performance and Erosion of the Project Objectives

In the event that it appears that a contract will not deliver the contracted scope, will be delivered so late that the business case will be invalidated or beneficial use will be substantially late, the employer may choose to terminate the contract. Each contract typically contains termination clauses to permit the employer (client) to terminate the employment of the contractor, commonly by reason of specified defaults (although some contracts can be terminated by their employer at any time and "at will", and will not be conditional upon some specified default). These defaults are typically termed as "material" breaches, which are defined in the contract and may relate to rate of progress, failure to deliver the scope, failure to comply with an instruction, breach of statutory regulations or suspension of the project. In addition, the employer normally stipulates that post-termination of the contractor, they will be permitted to bring in a second contractor to complete the works. If a "standard form" has been adopted (one published by a recognised body) which has not been modified (clauses, added, deleted or amended) and has already been tested in the courts, then employers and contractors can predict to some degree the outcome of a court case or arbitration. If the contract has been specifically written for the project or is a substantially modified standard form, the outcome of a dispute could expose the client to unknown risk. An example of a terminated project is the e-Borders contract described in Case Study 12, which became the subject of litigation.

CASE STUDY 12 – UK GOVERNMENT E-BORDERS CONTRACT, UK

On 22 July 2010, the Minister of State for Immigration, Damian Green, announced the cancellation of the contract with Raytheon Systems Limited,[1] the prime supplier for the government's e-Borders programme. The aim of the programme is to assist in reducing the threat of terrorist attacks, disrupt cross-border crime and prevent abuses of the immigration system. It is described as a key element of the government's strategy to deliver robust border controls and support the national counter-terrorism strategy. The project began in 2007. At the time of the cancellation of the contract, the government had spent £188 million on supplier costs against a total contract cost of around £750 million. The decision to cancel was made following a project review. At the time of review, progress of the programme had been considered to be "extremely disappointing". While some elements had been delivered, they have not been delivered on time. Delivery of the next critical part of the programme was already running at least 12 months late. Over and above this confirmed delay, there were risks of further delays. In addition, the government stated it had "no confidence in the current prime supplier ... being able to address this situation". The Minister disclosed that "it has been clear for some time that the way the existing programme was developing gave rise to serious concern". The government stated it would

---

1   Ministerial statement included on the Home Office website: https://www.gov.uk/government/speeches/cancellation-of-the-e-borders-contract.

appoint another supplier to complete the project. The cancellation calls into question whether the scope and schedule were realistic, whether the process adopted for tender evaluation was appropriate and whether the choice and capabilities of the prime supplier were sufficiently scrutinised. Following the cancellation, the parties went to arbitration to settle their differences, with both making a substantial claim for damages.

Contractor

Contractor selection plays a vital role in the overall success of a project. Poor contractor performance represents a very significant risk and can lead to a number of detrimental outcomes, including delays, emerging defects, reduced functionality or project cancellation. For construction projects, it can range from poor workmanship to late beneficial occupation and protracted contractual disputes. Increased costs and/or late delivery can negate a project's business case. Hence, selection criteria for construction contractors for both pre-qualification and tender evaluation require careful consideration and application. While contractor evaluation continues to receive close attention from construction researchers and practitioners alike, evaluation criteria themselves have remained essentially unchanged over the last decade. The emphasis remains on contractors' financial, managerial, technical, health and safety and quality capabilities combined with past performance. An example of where contractor selection did not take account of previous experience, typically a key criterion in any suitability assessment, is the FiReControl Project described in Case Study 13.

CASE STUDY 13 – THE FIRECONTROL PROJECT, ENGLAND

Despite the long preparation time, the IT contract itself was poorly designed and managed. The contract was awarded to a company with no direct experience of supplying the emergency services. The contractor mostly relied on subcontractors over which the Department for Communities and Local Government had no visibility or control. The contract did not include appropriate milestones to enable the Department to hold the contractor to account. The Department was also unable to terminate the IT contract without exposing itself to large costs. Payments within the contract were scheduled too late and created tension in an already poor relationship. The Department failed to ensure that the contractor followed the approach set out in the contract.

Procurement risk management should be a major concern for all those embarking on projects. Inappropriate and misguided choices can lead to significant overspend, delays and missed objectives.

5

Leadership

☑ **Senior management commitment to risk management needs to be visible**

> *Visible senior management support was one of six critical areas which contributed to programme success.*
>
> Elaine Davies, Eurostar Programme Office Manager (HS1)[1]

Do team members on your project know that senior management support the practice of risk management? If so, how do they know this? How and when was it communicated? While the discipline of risk management is now mature, its integration into projects is not automatic. While the inclusion of PRM as one of the nine knowledge areas in *A Guide to the Project Management Body of Knowledge* (*PMBOK Guide*)[2] published by PMI[3] has been of assistance, in many organisations and on many projects, the adoption of risk practices still has to be "sold". The merits of risk management have to be spelt out repeatedly. In many cases, successful risk management is dependent on the visibility of senior management's commitment to establishing a risk-conscious organisation – the "tone at the top" as it is commonly referred to these days. This visibility can apply to all aspects of project management, not just risk management (see Case Study 14 below). For risk management to be effective across a project, there needs to be a collective belief that risk management is a fruitful and a productive use of time, and that it will pay dividends in both

---

1   High Speed 1 (HS1), previously known as the Channel Tunnel Rail Link (CTRL), the UK's first major new railway in over a century: a high-speed line allowing trains to run at speeds of up to 300 km/h between the Channel Tunnel and London.

2   *A Guide to the Project Management Body of Knowledge* (*PMBOK Guide*) is a book which presents a set of standard terminology and guidelines for project management. The fourth edition (2008) was recognised by the American National Standards Institute (ANSI) as an American National Standard (ANSI/PMI 99-001-2008) and by the Institute of Electrical and Electronics Engineers (IEEE 1490-2011).

3   The PMI is a not-for-profit membership association for the project management profession, with more than 650,000 members and credential holders in more than 185 countries. Its worldwide advocacy for project management is supported by globally recognised standards and credentials, an extensive research programme and professional development initiatives.

the short and the long term. Human resource management adopts an analogy for explaining the creation of such a shared understanding. They describe the need for a process of "evangelisation", the process of winning acceptance through the organisation of a common purpose and a shared mission, and, in addition, that this shared mission is achieved through the broad adoption of certain processes and procedures. It is often referred to as the winning of hearts and minds, an idea that has been a common thread in management thinking for most of the twentieth century. Evangelisation works through three key concepts: "a shared belief", "apostles" and "parables".

CASE STUDY 14 – HIGH SPEED 1 (HS1), ENGLAND, UK

An example of a successful project is HS1, previously known as the Channel Tunnel Rail Link (CTRL), a high-speed line between London and UK end of the Channel Tunnel. Eurostar Chief Executive Officer Richard Brown not only championed the HS1 programme throughout, he also insisted that project management at Eurostar was "professionalised" before the programme commenced. Eurostar worked with a consultancy to review and strengthen its project management capability. Brown advised that: "The impact of this work focused us on performance and delivery, and created a 'profession' within the project management community. This was invaluable in helping us open services on HS1 from the new station at St Pancras International exactly on time and to a high standard." Appropriate authority was confidently delegated to the programme director, reducing bureaucratic delays, and HS1 was an agenda item at each main board meeting, giving it "visibility" and underwriting its status as a critical strategic initiative.

A shared belief: risk management requires the development of project homogeneity – a shared belief in how to implement a project. Homogeneity is created (it is suggested) by a number of factors, such as:

- recruiting staff with similar views and experiences;

- sharing a problem and its resolution;

- endogenous change arising from the view that "things" have to be done differently after a setback;

- recognising that a change to the previous way of doing things is required.[4]

CASE STUDY 15 – TERMINAL 5, HEATHROW AIRPORT, UK

The BAA[1] Terminal 5 project is a prime example of where a shared belief in risk management permeated the entire approach to project execution. BAA's refreshing and enlightened view of risk management is that "project management is the tool of the risk management approach not vice-versa".[2] Risk management informed the project delivery strategy, procurement route, form of contract, programming and cost control. At an organisational level, risk management was built into the plans and objectives for all of the project team. The significance of the project to BAA and particularly the need for robust risk management was clearly recognised. There was a clear appreciation by BAA that due to the scale of the project, cost overruns could have a material impact on its reputation, cashflow, balance sheet and future viability. Based on its experience of recent major projects, such as the Heathrow Expressway, BAA's view was that, no matter how risk was apparently placed under different forms of contract, the end result would be the same – the client still would bear and pay for risk. BAA's aim was to identify the sources of risk and then marshal and bring to bear the best resources possible in terms of managing them. "The T5 Agreement" was a cost-reimbursable form of contract, which ring-fenced suppliers' profits and assigned risk to the client. The contract focused on the causes of risk and on risk management through integrated team approaches. The contract was drafted in a non-adversarial style. The risk process identified the "root cause" of each risk, enabling risk responses to be specific and tailored. Where it was considered appropriate, responses to critical risks that had been identified sufficiently

---

1   BAA is the acronym retained from the time when the company was called the British Airports Authority. The name has been subsequently changed as the company was bought by the Spanish infrastructure company Ferrovial in 2006 (hence the "British" is no longer appropriate). In addition, as a result of competition laws, it has had to sell off many of its UK airports.

2   NAO (2005) *Case Studies: Improving Public Services through Better Construction*, Report by the Comptroller and Auditor General, HC 364-II, Session 2004–2005, 15 March 2005.

---

4   Examples of the implementation of change management to bring about the introduction of new programme management techniques were the practices introduced by Eurostar for HS1. As explained by Jane Marshall-Nichols of consultants CITI: "When it came to facilitating change management, buy-in by staff was a critical factor, driving many management actions. It was integral to the smooth transition to the new services that a pragmatic set of management actions were in place to handle the hard core of staff who were antagonistic and unwilling to participate in the programme. A central change management plan covering all aspects and events was also developed by change management professionals who were hired to manage and resource this critical area."

> early on in the programme were tested in advance in order to determine their effectiveness. An example is where the T5 roof team, including the designers, suppliers and fabricators, pre-erected the roof abutment structure off-site in Yorkshire to gain a greater appreciation of the challenge of erecting the huge roof (which spans more than 150 metres). The pilot identified 140 significant lessons. Each finding had a unique risk mitigation plan, enabling faster construction on-site. Overall, the project team estimated that at least three months were saved by this pre-emptive risk management approach. In this particular case, the time saved enabled delays that had previously arisen during the wet winter of 2001–2 to be recovered and the project to be kept on track.

Apostles: the apostles are ambassadors for risk management who are members of senior management. These ambassadors hold senior positions, are highly visible on the project and frequently meet with the CEO and the Project Director. Their primary goal is to "spread the word" on risk management. They:

- advocate the adoption of risk management;

- explain the PRM policy;

- justify the use of risk management practices;

- counter prejudices, jaundiced views and parochial thinking;

- help the development of the field of risk management;

- promulgate the adherence to risk management practices so that they become the norm;

- publicly support members of the risk management team;

- overcome project team resistance where discipline leads consider that risk management intrudes into what they consider to be their own preserve. For instance, risk management questions the choice of contract, the method of assessing the impact of change, the basis of costs, the duration of programme activities and the response to contractor performance.

Parables: parables are used to reinforce the view that risk management adds value. Parables are success stories.[5] They are accounts of where risk management has contributed to avoiding a potential problem or problems, such aiding decision making or taking the project on a different path from that adopted on other projects and thus avoiding commonly occurring problems. Parables can be communicated in many ways:

- articles in a newsletter;

- wide circulation emails;

- posters on noticeboards;

- lunchtime seminars;

- academic papers and professional magazine articles;

- an introduction at meetings, presentations and workshops;

- case studies.

> It needs to be seen that risk management has senior management support. Risk management can only be delivered from the top down, not from the bottom up.

---

5   Principle f) of ISO 31000 entitled "Risk management is based on the best available information" states that: "The inputs to the process of managing risk are based on information sources such as historical data, experience, stakeholder feedback, observation, forecasts and expert judgment. Success stories are based on those that have experience of completed projects."

6

Internal Stakeholders

☑ **Risk management must include an assessment of internal stakeholders**

> *As managers must take decisions in an uncertain environment, there is a direct link between risk, uncertainty and performance.*
>
> *Alex Dali,*
> *President of the Global Institute for Risk Management Standards*

The simple definition of internal stakeholders adopted here is that they are those individuals within a project organisation who will initiate the project, sanction expenditure, agree the scope, participate in implementation and use the output. In a broader sense, stakeholders are those who will influence the project it or be affected by it. Who these stakeholders are will vary to some degree between projects in the public and private sectors and from industry to industry. The internal stakeholders of a project may include the project board, customer, end users, project manager, project team and in-house functions such as finance, legal, information technology, public relations and human resources. The customer and the end user may be from the same organisation or different organisations. When from the same organisation, they may be from different parts of the organisation, such as from within a subsidiary, division, group or department. The way in which the internal stakeholders work together will be the source of both project uncertainty and opportunity.

Determinants of Internal Stakeholder Effectiveness

A structure that may be used to understand the drivers behind effective internal stakeholder management as well as their inherent sources of uncertainty is the determinants of group effectiveness proposed by Charles Handy.[1] A group is treated here as a project organisation composed of internal stakeholders

---

1   Handy, C. (1981) *Understanding Organisations*. Harmondsworth: Penguin Books.

where the members have: common objectives, a common identity (such as a project name), a unique role and use common procedures, software (such as a document database) and information technology. The structure is divided into the "givens", the "intervening factors" and the "outcomes". The "givens" can be altered in the long or medium term, but are constraints within which the group has to operate within the short term. The "intervening factors" are those aspects of the group that can be changed in the short term, taking account of the "givens". The "outcomes" are the measures of group success. A visual representation of the structure is included in Figure 6.1. The elements numbered one to eight are explained briefly below.

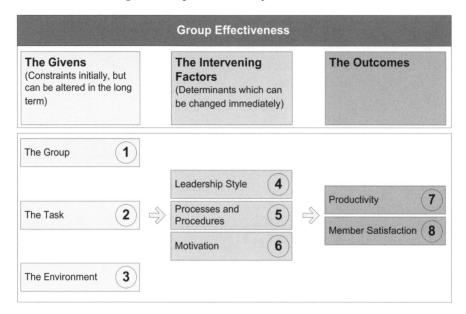

Figure 6.1   Determinants of group effectiveness based on Handy (1981)

The Givens

1. The group: the group "givens" are the size, member characteristics, individual objectives and stage of development (maturity or growth cycle of the group).

2. The task: the task "givens" are the nature of the task, the criteria for effectiveness, the salience of the task and the clarity of the task.

3. The environment: the environment "givens" are the norms and expectations, the leader position, the inter-group relations and the physical location.

The Intervening Factors

1. Leadership style: numerous approaches have been proposed by academics, including trait, style and contingency theories of leadership. Handy promotes an extension of the contingency theory called the "best-fit approach", whereby leader and subordinate styles and demands of the task are aligned on the continuum between tight (structured) and flexible (supportive).

2. Processes and procedures: these factors cover task functions and maintenance functions.

3. Motivation: motivation will be driven by knowledge of expected results, standards to be achieved, individuals desire to realise a sense of achievement and the collective desire to be successful.

The Outcomes

1. Productivity: productivity for projects may be measured in terms of the outturn completion date and intermediate milestones being met, the project scope being satisfied and the required quality standards being adhered to.

2. Member satisfaction: this will be accomplished if the end users consider that their requirements have been met, the project sponsors believe they have obtained value for money, the relationship with external stakeholders has not been tarnished and the maintainer has not been saddled with higher-than-expected life-cycle costs.

The Givens

Of the "givens" within Charles Handy's structure of group effectiveness, "the group" is considered here to be one of the greatest sources of uncertainty. The group (project organisation) will be a constraint that the sponsoring organisation will initially have to live with, whereas the intervening factors may be changed at short notice. Handy describes four characteristics of the group, namely the "size", "member characteristics", "individual objectives" and "stage of development". These are discussed in turn below.

Group (Project Organisation) Size

As projects grow in scale and complexity, so do the project organisations required to implement them. Project organisation size is also in part due to the proliferation of professional specialisations and a large project with over 25 different disciplines has now become the norm rather than the exception. The number of project team members and the degree of differentiated skills present a number of challenges in terms of internal stakeholder management. In particular, it entails engaging the right disciplines at the right time and to the right degree in each of the project life-cycle stages.

Member Characteristics

Where the execution of the scope is to be undertaken by internal stakeholders within the project organisation, there must be a timely assessment of their competencies (skills, experience and management capabilities) as well as their capacity (resources – finance, people and tools such as software). In particular, there needs to be a focus on programme, project and risk management capabilities. Specific capabilities are required in scope definition, programming and value management together with cost, change, quality and document control. Member characteristics cannot be changed in the short term; in other words, members cannot suddenly acquire several years of experience. However, it is recognised that some software skills can be obtained in the short term.

Individual Objectives

Where project team members have the same objectives, they will tend to be far more effective. However, commonly people bring hidden agendas to teams which often have nothing to do with the declared objectives of the team. Ignoring team politics can represent a significant risk to a project's health and longevity. Regrettably, projects can be used as pawns within a "game" of politics, undermining their performance. Project team politics can be described as the use of power within a project in the pursuit of agendas and forms of self-interest with disregard to their effect on the project's goals and the activities undertaken to achieve those goals. Power may be held through position, delegated authority, resources, expertise, knowledge, coercion, interpersonal skills and the operation of group dynamics. Power may be exercised across imperceptible hierarchies, as opposed to the formal visible hierarchies of authority – established for the execution of functions, management of resources and lines of reporting. These barely discernable hierarchies can result in decisions that were unexpected, that reverse earlier approvals, that appear counter-productive or that are contrary to the project's interests. While their image may improve, they may never come fully into focus. They constitute what many call the "shadow project organisation". These hierarchies are detected by noticing who is involved at the hub of social interactions and similarly who is the source of project intelligence. Team members emerge from the shadow organisation when it is apparent who has influence, who is respected and who champions others. A visual map may be created, incorporating who is providing the direction (not just driving the bus). Each primary interrelationship may be noted, together with its strength of connection. The use of power is exhibited on the political landscape of a project. The political landscape might be described as the overall term for the hierarchy that links the political players together and defines their relationships at a particular point in time. The main link between individuals on a political landscape is the access to information before others that they may use for personal gain and advancement rather than securing the project's goals.

Stage of Development

The importance of the project to the organisation may be perceived differently by the different contributing elements of the organisation. One of the most vital characteristics of an effective project is internal stakeholder collaboration. This collaboration can be at various levels in the organisation, such as between divisions, departments or team members (who may be drawn from different departments). Understandably, a considerable amount has been written about the behaviour and characteristics of teams, as their performance has a direct correlation with project outcomes. An extreme example of judging, understanding and responding to the risks that may emanate from internal stakeholders and specifically team members are the risk practices undertaken for projects which take expeditions into the relatively unknown. As mentioned in Case Study 16, building a team with the right character and attitude was considered to be of paramount importance. A team member's very survival could depend on the capabilities and behaviours of his/her team members.

CASE STUDY 16 – THE COLDEST JOURNEY, ANTARCTICA

Projects can take many forms. This project consists of a record-breaking attempt by Sir Ranulph Fiennes and five other explorers to cross Antarctica in winter from the Russian base of Novolazarevskaya via the South Pole to Captain Scott's base at McMurdo Sound, a distance of more than 2,000 miles. The project will be completed mostly in darkness. The British Antarctic Territory is the UK's largest overseas territory. The UK has the longest established claim to territory in the Antarctic, dating back to 1908. The Territory is administered by the Foreign & Commonwealth Office's (FCO) Polar Regions Department. The Director of the Overseas Territories Directorate acts as Commissioner, and the Head of the Polar Regions Department as the Deputy Commissioner. Commencement was delayed by five years until the UK Foreign and Commonwealth Office granted a permit for the project to proceed. Permits are issued by the FCO's Polar Regions Department. Permit applications must meet a strict set of conditions and in particular must satisfy the Polar Regions Department that the expedition will be safe and environmentally friendly. The expedition was initially refused permission as it had been deemed far too risky and the chances of disaster too high. The average winter temperature at the South Pole is – minus 60°C, which is also the temperature at which inhalation of air can cause irreparable damage to the lungs. This decision was only overturned after it was shown that technological innovations could mitigate some of the major risks of the crossing. On 7 January 2013, Sir Ranulph and his crew left Cape Town aboard the South African polar vessel, the *SA Agulhas*. His destination was again Antarctica. On 21 March 2013, the six-man team set off from Crown Bay in Antarctica on their record-breaking attempt to do the unthinkable. There is no ambiguity; attempting to cross the continent in winter exposes the expedition to very high risks and completing the challenge will require extraordinary stamina, endurance and determination. Sir Ranulph has described the enormous challenge of finding the right volunteers and planning journeys of immense complexity beset by political, personal, geographical, financial and physical obstacles. Building a team with the right character and attitude is considered to be of paramount importance. Persistence, tolerance, fitness, agility and the ability to perform under extreme pressure are all necessary characteristics of team members who are highly dependent on each other. In addition, it is vitally important that all team members share a common goal and do not seek to pursue hidden agendas.

The maturity of the stage of development of the team will influence the proficiency and effectiveness of the communication between the internal stakeholders as a whole and in particular between individual team members. Communication with stakeholders must be throughout the PLC, as indicated in Figure 6.2.

Communication may take a number of forms, depending on the size and structure of the organisation and the number and location of the stakeholders. Examples of the types of communication that may be adopted are also included in Figure 6.2. These communications may also include copies of documents shared with external stakeholders or press releases issued to inform the public.

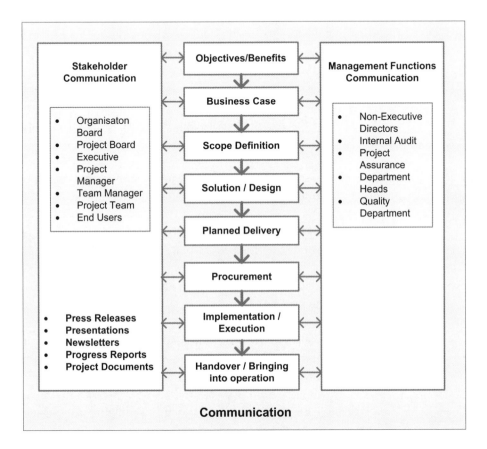

Figure 6.2   Internal stakeholder communication

Internal Stakeholder Risks

The risks associated with internal stakeholder management are considerable and will be strongly influenced by the organisation's evolution, culture, structure and dominant personalities. Included below are some of the more common risks:

- Failure to identify a stakeholder, leading to missing requirements.

- Lack of alignment of stakeholder requirements.

- Failure to effectively communicate with stakeholders, leading to missed requirements.

- Inability of stakeholders to work effectively together.

- Failure to keep all project stakeholders appraised of the project's progress at the same time.

- Lack of prompt resolution of conflicting stakeholder requirements, leading to delays in scope definition.

- Requirement to scale down end-user requirements as they were not aligned to the budget during project requirements capture.

- Lack of willingness of stakeholders to perform the activities assigned to them during the project planning stage.

- Organisational politics where personal agendas are pursued to the detriment of the project:

  - Conscious exclusion of a stakeholder from involvement in the development of the business case to avoid the merit of the project being challenged or project cancellation.

  - Frustrated employees lashing out by sabotaging co-workers through withholding information.

  - Distracted employees spending more time worrying about which way the office wind is blowing than focusing on their own responsibilities.

  - Good employees tiring of co-worker behaviour and leaving the company, taking their skills and ethics with them.

  - Resistance by a single stakeholder to the project due to concerns over job security.

    –   Objections to the project by a stakeholder group as it will divert funding from their own project.

    –   Lobbying of stakeholders by an individual stakeholder to delay or abandon the project due to concerns over maintaining their position in the organisation hierarchy.

- Lack of involvement of stakeholders throughout the PLC. This may be at gate reviews, key approval stages or when the business case is modified. This may result in the withholding of approval and/or resources at a late stage in the project when stakeholders are apprised of the current status of the project.

> How effectively internal stakeholders work together will have a direct bearing on project outcomes, warranting both scrutiny and management of working group risks.

☑ Involve internal stakeholders in evaluation of the risks to the business case

> *Our focus on meaningful projects means serving a useful social purpose while generating high-quality profits.*
> *Masimi Iijima, President and CEO, Mitsui & Co., Ltd*

A good business case provides internal stakeholders with the evidence to support their decision making and provides assurance to external stakeholders that they have acted responsibly. The business case process must involve the close scrutiny of all relevant financial and non-financial aspects of a proposed project (including its risk exposure) to ensure that the best possible solution is selected for a given set of circumstances. Frequently, many projects, particularly those in the public sector, fail to achieve their objectives and deliver anticipated benefits because the key phases of the investment have been inadequately scoped or planned and the associated risks have not been taken into account. Project success will in part be dependent on when the internal stakeholders are engaged in the preparation, review and sanction of the business case, and how well they understand and apply the concepts of risk management in their decision making.

Project Definition

Generally speaking, efficient project development requires project stakeholders' needs to be translated into technical solutions within the constraints of, for example, finance, timelines, planning legislation, quality parameters and risk exposure. This argues for measured incremental development by way of *engaging with the internal project stakeholders* to define and effectively articulate the strategic objectives, define the scope, evaluate options, assess capital, operating and maintenance costs, and analyse and manage risk. A key communication tool which captures and aids the dissemination of these critical development activities is the business case. This is the tool that enables internal stakeholders to evaluate the risks against the planned benefits and decide whether or not to sanction project investment.

Significance of the Business Case

Allport et al.'s research[2] of urban transportation projects states that "the business case should be the central document that provides clarity as to the project's purpose, scope, risks, impacts and intended outcomes. It facilitates consultation with key stakeholders (by avoiding ambiguity) and so far as possible needs to be agreed by them". The authors expand on the significance of the business case by their remarks that "the business case should be developed from the earliest stage of project development and modified continuously". The UK project management methodology PRINCE2[3] describes the business case as the most important document on the project. It answers the question:

---

2   Allport, R., Brown, R., Glaister, S. and Travers, T. (2008) "Success and Failure in Urban Transport Infrastructure Projects". The research examined 22 transportation project case studies from around the world. The research was sponsored by the KPMG.

3   *Managing Successful Projects with PRINCE2*, 2005 edn. London: The Stationery Office, on behalf of the OGC. The PRINCE (PRojects IN Controlled Environments) was first established in 1989 by the UK CCTA (Central Computer and Telecommunications Agency). The CCTA (which became the UK Office of Government Commerce) continued to develop the method and PRINCE2 was launched in 1996 in response to user requirements for improved guidance on project management on all projects, not just information systems. The OGC declared in its foreword to *Managing Successful Projects with PRINCE2* that PRINCE2 is "recognised as a world-class international product and is the standard method for project management ... and provides a flexible and adaptable approach to suit all projects". It is used extensively by the UK government as well as having been widely adopted in the private sector. The methodology describes a formal and highly structured delivery method composed of a number of discrete stages supported by a number of project disciplines, such as planning and quality (described as components).

"Why should this project be undertaken?" A project's business case provides all stakeholders with basic information about the project. It describes the overall reasons and business justification for a project's implementation, based on its costs, risks and benefits. A project which failed due the lack of a business case was the Jubilee Line extension implemented in the UK. The consequence of the lack of preparation of a business case is emphasised by researchers Allport et al., who consider its omission as one of the main reasons why the project did not achieve its objectives (see Case Study 17 below).

CASE STUDY 17 – JUBILEE LINE EXTENSION (JLE), LONDON, UK

The evolution of the JLE project was complex in terms of financing, promotion and number of stakeholders. A window on the project is provided by the report prepared by Ove Arup Partnership Limited appointed by the Department of Environment, Transport and the Regions as the "Secretary of State's Agent" to provide "impartial and expert advice on the construction phase of the Project and make objective reviews of the JLE Project meeting its cost and programme targets". Arup's End-of-Commission Report[1] provides an independent and authoritative view of actual events: "When the go-ahead for construction was given, [the] targets were for completion in 53 months and within an approved budget of £2.1 bn. When the works were completed in December 1999, it had taken 74 months (40 per cent more), and the final forecast cost had risen to £3.5 bn. (67 per cent more)." This included some items not included in the "go-ahead" budget. The project has never met its objectives in terms of train frequency and reliability. It was clear from the Arup report that there was no clear business case, which is thought to be the reason behind the ill-defined scope and changing sponsors/leadership, which in turn led to considerable scope creep. The absence of a business case denied decision makers the ability to adequately define, assess and communicate the project risks.

---

1   Arup, "End-of-Commission Report", July 2000.

Format of the Business Case

There are many formats in use in terms of the content of a business case. The content proposed by PRINCE2 includes why the project is needed, the options that have been appraised, the benefits expected, a summary of the high-level threats, an outline of the costs and the timeline, an investment appraisal and an evaluation of the claimed benefits and the investment proposal. The underpinning philosophy of PRINCE2 is that once the business case has been agreed, it must drive all the project management processes throughout the PLC, from initial start-up through to successful completion. This is accomplished by being reviewed by the project sponsor at each of the key intermediate decision points. The importance of this review is emphasised by the erudite authors of the methodology, who state that: "When setting up and particularly while the project is running, it is all too easy to concentrate on *what* is being done and *how* it is being done, while ignoring *why* it needs to be done. The Business Case states *why* the work is being done and as such is a crucial element of the project." In essence, it describes the benefits sought and how these will support the organisation (or, for public projects, the wider socio-economic benefits). An example of a project where realistic achievable project benefits were clearly articulated to support the business case is given in Case Study 18 below.

CASE STUDY 18 – DIAMOND SYNCHROTRON, UK

The Diamond Light Source is a new scientific facility located within the renowned Harwell Science and Innovation Campus near Didcot, Oxfordshire. A truly fascinating project, it is housed in a giant doughnut-shaped, steel-clad building covering an area in excess of 43,300 square metres. It is the largest UK-funded scientific facility to have been built in over 40 years. It houses the synchrotron, which contains three particle accelerators that are used to produce extremely bright beams of x-rays, infrared and ultra-violet light – called "synchrotron light". These beams are around 100 billion times brighter than a standard hospital X-ray machine or 10 billion times brighter than the sun. The ring is not circular, but is shaped as a 24-sided polygon. Electrons are accelerated around the large "storage ring" to just under the speed of light. As the electrons pass through specially designed magnets at each vertex, their sudden change of direction causes them to emit exceptionally bright beams of light. This light can be transferred into one of the experimental laboratories (or beamlines) found at points along the ring and used to study a variety of materials. The business case for the Diamond Synchrotron[1] presented the following information to support judgment on the scientific benefits:

- the range of scientific enquiry being pursued using synchrotron radiation;
- the current size of the UK user community, depending on the existing synchrotron radiation source;

---

1   NAO (2007) *Strengthening the Preparation of Project Proposals: Large Scientific Facilities*, in association with the Department for Innovation, Universities & Skills and Research Councils UK. National Audit Office, November.

- the level of peer-supported demand for access to the existing synchrotron radiation source;
- the number of publications arising from use of the existing synchrotron radiation source and UK use of the European Synchrotron Radiation Facility machine;
- the achievements from UK exploitation of synchrotron radiation to date;
- the future fields of research which will benefit from access to synchrotron radiation;
- the outcome of a survey of the UK life science community's estimates of its future demand for access to synchrotron radiation;
- the outcome of user consultations on anticipated requirements for availability of synchrotron radiation;
- the projections of funding agencies requirements for the availability of synchrotron radiation.

Evidence-Based Decision Making

Business cases are developed in the UK public sector in line with HM Treasury's advice on evidence-based decision making set out in the Green Book and use its best-practice five-case model approach.

This approach shows whether schemes:

- are supported by a robust case for change that fits with wider public policy objectives – the "strategic case";

- are commercially viable – the "commercial case";

- are financially affordable – the "financial case";

- are achievable – the "management case"; and

- demonstrate value for money – the "economic case".

Strategic case: the strategic case describes the project background and, most importantly, the project objectives and the critical success factors to satisfy the objectives.

Commercial case: the commercial case describes whether the project is commercially feasible, the procurement strategy, the form of contract and any key contractual issues (such as key milestones or key access dates).

Financial case: the financial case describes the affordability, sources of funding and the financing of cost overruns.

Management case: the management case describes the practicality of the delivery of the project and the need as appropriate for project management and accompanying planning, cost, change, contingency, value, procurement, stakeholder and integration management, together with gate reviews and project assurance.

Economic case: the economic case describes a long list of options based on wide consultation which subsequently will be reduced to a shortlist for further comparison, eliminating those that do not justify further consideration. Recommended practice suggests the options must include the "do nothing" or "do minimum" option. Alternatives will be compared, taking into consideration:

- all costs (including their source and any related assumptions), such as capital investment cost, estimated whole life or running costs (including disposal where this is expected to be significant), project management costs (both internal and external), design costs, construction costs, costs of plant, equipment, furniture and fittings, costs of staff to run and administer the facility, rent, utilities, insurance, security, repairs and maintenance, and decommissioning costs;

- contingency sums;

- quantified anticipated benefits;

- the ultimate disposal value (if any);

- adjustment of capital and operating costs to take account of optimism bias;

- identified risks, constraints and dependencies.

In terms of risk management, the internal stakeholders must:

- ascertain whether the benefits will be significantly greater than the costs (capital and operational) and the delivery risks;

- have a good comprehension of the major threats facing the project and the degree to which they may be mitigated;

- comprehend the regulatory context of the project and the adverse events that may arise from delayed approvals or onerous conditions;

- understand the anticipated allocation of threats and opportunities through the procurement route, choice of contract, contract conditions and selection of insurance policies;

- have given consideration to how the project's threat exposure may change over time (particularly where projects span several years and may be influenced by the external environment);

- gain information to "bottom-out" assumptions as soon as possible;

- understand the robustness of the capital expenditure cost plan and the confidence that can be placed in it;

- establish if the procurement option analysis is risk-based;

- discern the appropriateness of the contingency and establish if it is risk-based.

A project which failed due to the omission of stakeholder engagement, identification of the primary risks and completion of a business case was the FiReControl Project in the UK. The UK House of Commons review considered that the prime reason why the FiReControl Project failed was that it did not engage with the key stakeholders to debate, agree and finalise the content of the business case prior to commencement of the project (see the continuation of Case Study 13 below). In particular, it did not involve the end users in the development of the business case or the identification of potential threats to the project's objectives. Hence, there was no buy-in to a business case from end users before the physical work commenced. They did not agree to its purpose, scope or operation. There was also an under-appreciation of the risks and unrealistic optimism with regard to the deliverability of the IT solution. It is difficult to fathom why this project was "railroaded" through.

CASE STUDY 13 (CONTINUED) – THE FIRECONTROL PROJECT, ENGLAND[1]

This project is an example of where the business case was not prepared and agreed with the key stakeholders before rushing headlong into delivery, with very adverse consequences. The UK Department for Communities and Local Government (the "Department") embarked on the FiReControl Project in 2004. Its aim was to modernise the Fire Service in the wake of the 9/11 attacks, the 2002 Bain Review[2] and the proposal to establish regional fire services in England, as outlined in the 2003 White Paper *Our Fire and Rescue Service*. The objective of FiReControl was to improve national resilience, efficiency and technology by replacing the control room functions of 46 local Fire and Rescue Services in England with a network of nine purpose-built regional control centres using a national computer system. The project was launched in 2004, but, following a series of delays and difficulties, was terminated in December 2010, with none of the original objectives being achieved and a minimum of £469 million having being spent. Eight of the purpose-built regional control centres remain empty and continue to cost the taxpayer £4 million per month to maintain. A key failing of the project was that the Department, rather than engaging with the Services to persuade them of the project's merits, excluded them from decisions about the rationale for the project, the design of the regional control centres and the proposed IT solution. As reported by the House of Commons, as a consequence of the fast pace of project implementation, insufficient attention was paid to analysing the costs or understanding the risks to the project. In fact, the project was approved by the Department and the Treasury before a project plan or business case was finalised.

---

1 House of Commons Committee of Public Accounts (2011) *The Failure of the FiReControl Project*, Fiftieth Report of Session 2010–12, ordered by the House of Commons, printed 14 September.

2 "The Future of the Fire Service: Reducing Risk, Saving Lives", independent review of the Fire Service, December 2002, available at: http://www.fitting-in.com/reports/strikebainetc/bain report.pdf.

An example of a project which benefited from investing the time to develop and refine the business case through wide-ranging stakeholder involvement, in order to understand the scope and the attendant threats to the project's objectives, was the Channel Deepening Project described in Case Study 19.

CASE STUDY 19 – CHANNEL DEEPENING PROJECT, VICTORIA, AUSTRALIA

The Port of Melbourne (PoM) is one of Australia's largest container ports and its operation is critical to the economic well-being of Victoria. It handles more shipping containers than any other Australian port and is linked to the open sea by shipping channels running through Port Phillip Bay. The Channel Deepening Project was one of the largest and most critical maritime projects undertaken in Victoria. It primarily involved dredging specific shipping channels in Port Phillip Bay to deepen them and thus accommodate larger vessels with heavier cargo loads. Dredging commenced in February 2008 and was completed in November 2009, one month ahead of the project deadline and at least $200 million below its budget of $969 million. The project's risk contingency was $137 million,[1] which indicates that the overall cost savings were attributable to strong risk mitigation by the PoM project. Throughout the planning phase of the project, the PoM Corporation developed revised versions of the business case to accommodate changes in costs, environmental requirements and project scope. While the business case development process was iterative, time-consuming and required a significant commitment of resources, it ultimately led to a robust comprehensive business case. This comprehensive business case provided enough information to enable the government of Victoria to approve the project and ensured that the project was well designed and scoped, which contributed to its successful delivery. The Victorian Auditor-General's Office audit of the project undertaken in early 2009 found that the final business case complied with the requirements of the Victorian business case guidelines by providing evidence of wide-ranging stakeholder consultation, following a sound approach in deciding on a preferred option and explaining the approach to managing risks. Nick Easy, Executive General Manager of the Channel Deeping Project, noted that "putting in the work to understand the project scope and its risks (in a dynamic environment) was critical to the PoM Corporation developing robust project controls and effective risk management strategies[2] – which ultimately led to a well-managed successful outcome".[3]

---

1 Victorian Auditor-General's Office, *The Channel Deepening Project*, May 2009, available at: http://download.audit.vic.gov.au/files/Channel_Deepening_Report.pdf.
2 Principle j) of ISO 31000, "Risk management is dynamic, iterative and responsive to change", states that "Risk management continually senses and responds to change".
3 Australian Government, Department of Infrastructure and Transport (2010) *Infrastructure Planning and Delivery: Best Practice Case Studies*.

The effectiveness of risk management will be influenced by the degree to which internal stakeholders involve themselves in understanding the risks to the business case.

☑ Inculcating risk is improved by convincing the sceptics

> *No construction project is risk-free. Risk can be managed, minimised,*
> *shared, transferred or accepted. It cannot be ignored.*
>
> Sir Michael Latham,
> *former Member of Parliament and*
> *Chairman of the Construction Industry Board*

While there is a plethora of books, academic papers and articles on the subject of project risk management, few publications face up to the problems that typically confront the risk manager. Many shy away from the unspoken truth that many project teams or project managers are sceptical about the value of risk management. The discipline is not fully understood. Some consider it to be highly subjective, little more than just guesswork and tedious to undertake. It involves spending precious time on events that may never occur. Team members do not turn up for meetings, arrive late, leave early or spend most of their time reading emails on their mobile phones. Individual project members complain that risk management reduces the time available to do the "real work". They have not worked on a project where they have seen risk management make a difference. Frequently, the risk manager is expected to work on projects part-time, leading to superficial attention to identification, analysis and response planning. In addition, software necessary for data management or quantitative analysis is purchased late or not at all. This all sounds very bleak and is possibly all too familiar to the seasoned risk manager. There is no magic wand which will remove all of these problems. If you speak to any manager in any specialist professional occupation, he/she will be faced with similar problems of lack of engagement, motivation, culture, awareness, collaboration or team working.

However, you ignore the sceptics at your peril. Left unchecked, sceptics can dissuade project team members from engaging in risk management and can drain the risk team's morale. Sceptics' vocalised lack of belief in risk management and their reticence to engage in risk processes can seriously undermine the risk management team's commitment and enthusiasm to deliver effective risk management. The worst sceptics are those in senior positions who "infect" the team beneath them. Then it becomes a constant uphill struggle to gain project team participation in risk management.

How do you know who the sceptics are? Some will be blatantly obvious by their remarks, while others will emerge over time when they repeatedly accept meeting invites, but do not appear, are slow to respond to emails or fail to contribute risk information.

Our biggest sceptics remain the oldest hands that got to where they are without risk management and see no need to introduce new disciplines now. One senior project manager confided to a risk manager that he did not believe in risk management. He later shared with the risk manager that his reluctance to get involved in risk management was based on his belief that he was "too old to learn new tricks". A senior manager on the same project said "the client has not been asking for risk reports so we have not being preparing them" (this is despite the fact that the contract signed with the client stipulated the provision of risk management and regular risk reports). When the client changed his executive director on the project, the new director quickly called for regular risk meetings and reports, and insisted on the timely definition and implementation of response actions to the most serious risks.

As discussed in Case Study 20, one way to combat sceptics is to provide examples of risk management successes and the ramifications of risk management failure. These can be examples from both international events in the public eye and from completed projects. A recent risk management success has been the Olympic Games held in London 2012. The London Organising Committee (LOCOG) and the International Olympic Committee (IOC) spent years thinking about adverse risk events. Simulations of security incidents were rehearsed and contingency plans for mass evacuations or emergency situations were put in place. Consideration was given to a terrorist incident, a breakdown of the London rail system, power blackouts, volcanic ash clouds, flooding and an outbreak of an infectious disease. Risk management is now at the centre of the governance model for the Olympic Games and the Olympic movement, and not only because of their growing scale and complexity, but also due to the timeframe involved. The time between the winning city's bid to the opening ceremony can be many years, leading to greater vulnerability to emerging risks emanating from a variety of resources, such as security, public health, natural ecology, technology and fluctuations in the economy.

CASE STUDY 20 – NAVAL SEA SYSTEMS COMMAND, USA[1]

US Naval Sea Systems Command (NAVSEA) established the Carrier Team One (CT1) organisation for defining, championing and improving the planning and executing of aircraft carrier overhauls. CT1 specifically provides the structure for managing and improving cost, time and quality performance of the execution processes. As a consequence of two aircraft carrier overhauls being a number of weeks late in 2006, CT1 formed a Risk Management Working Group (RMWG) and tasked the group to develop a standard risk management process that could be applied consistently across all aircraft carrier shipyards and support and monitor a risk management pilot to be implemented on nine carrier overhauls at five different locations over a one-year period. CT1 adopted the existing Northrop Grumman Shipbuilding Newport News Operations (NGSB-NN) risk management programme developed for aircraft carrier overhauls. The RMWG leader met with key stakeholders to share their procedures and develop their implementation plan. Early on in the pilot, team leaders wanted to see the value before engaging. In fact, resistance to implementing risk management occurred in all the projects within the pilot. To embed the discipline, risk management was integrated into command briefings, progress briefings, meeting agendas, team training, awards and recognition, newsletter articles, project strategies and lessons-learned meetings at the completion of the project. Data gathered during the pilot showed that project teams that embraced the formal risk management practice quickly achieved risk exposure reductions similar to those achieved by NGSB-NN teams that had been using it for years. Following the pilot, feedback from the project's leadership indicated that they were appreciative of the tool's ability to communicate and mitigate their biggest concerns. Matt Durkin, Norfolk Naval Shipyard's project superintendent for *USS Harry S Truman*'s 2009 overhaul, commented that "Risk Management provided me with more visibility of our project's key issues. I am not sure we would have completed our last availability (overhaul) on time without the RM process". In addition, Tim Ferguson, Puget Sound Naval Shipyard and Intermediate Facility's project superintendent for *USS Abraham Lincoln*'s 2009 overhaul, said: "Our project team leveraged the risk management program to support open and honest discussion of issues that could have impacted delivering the ship on time." The process is now being rolled out to all the US Navy's ships. As advised by Cleve Butts, NAVSEA's Director of Carrier Support: "It is absolutely essential that we complete our maintenance periods on time and within cost, not only for aircraft carriers but for all our ships. Risk Management is a great communication and management tool for ensuring that the right actions are being applied effectively and early. The RM (risk management) process has now been successfully implemented at all aircraft carrier shipyards."

---

1   This Case Study is based on the the following article: Fontaine, Dan (2012) "A Carrier Team One Risk Management Success Story", *Ask Magazine*, 37–41, available at: http://www.nasa.gov/offices/oce/appel/ask/issues/40/40s_carrier.html.

On new projects, the opportunity exists to share reports of events that occurred in previous projects where risk management made an irrefutable contribution to removing or reducing risk exposure. These events should be drawn from projects in the same industry and from the same project type, and should be from across the PLC, so that the sceptics cannot say "well, that example does not apply here". These historical events should be augmented by statements from published reports on project performance. Included below are a number of publications listed in chronological order that all emphasise the significance of risk management to successful project delivery:

- The 1999 National Audit Office report *Modernising Construction* highlighted inadequate use and understanding of risk management as a major barrier to improvement in construction performance.

- While NASA[4] has had some stunning successes with its space exploration programme, following the determination of the cause for the 1999 loss of the Mars Climate Orbiter, the mishap investigation board reviewed eight previous failure investigation reports and identified a correlation between other project failures together with a number of common themes. The themes included inadequate project reviews, poor risk management, insufficient testing and inadequate communication.[5]

- A paper entitled "How Poor Project Governance Causes Selays", presented to the Society of Construction Law, describes the failure of Metronet[6] as an example of poor corporate governance and cites poor risk identification and management as a contributing factor.[7] The authors of the paper go onto say that: "Our experience is that project risks that can lead to failure in delivery are most effectively mitigated in organisations where there are strong people competencies and effective management systems."

---

4   National Aeronautics and Space Administration.
5   Brady, T.K. (2002) "Utilization of Dependency Structure Matrix Analysis to Assess Implementation of NASA's Complex Technical Projects", submitted to the System Design and Management Program in Partial fulfilment of the Requirements for the Degree of Master of Science in Engineering and Management at the Massachusetts Institute of Technology.
6   Metronet was a consortium that won two of the three Public-Private Partnership (PPP) contracts with London Underground Limited (LUL) in 2003 for the maintenance and upgrade of two-thirds of the lines on LUL.
7   Morgan, A. and Gbedemah S. (2010) "How Poor Project Governance Causes Delays", paper presented to the Society of Construction Law.

- In 2003 the Major Project's Association seminar entitled "Learning from Project Failures" identified 10 reasons why projects fail, one of which included "inadequate risk identification".

- The OGC guide *Achieving Excellence in Construction Procurement Guide 05: The Integrated Project Team: Teamworking and Partnering*, published in 2003, lists seven project critical success factors. The first factor "for overall project success" it recorded as "a shared risk register, with risks allocated and managed across the team".

- The 2004 Association for Project Management (APM) publication *Directing Change: A Guide to Governance of Project Management* identifies 11 principles for effective project governance, one of which refers to the need for establishing criteria for the escalation of risk within the organisation.

- The National Audit Office publication *Managing Risks to Improve Public Services*, published in October 2004, states that improving risk management is a key government priority and records that: "Many failures in service delivery have arisen from a lack of effective risk identification and management. This has often resulted in poorly thought through plans, unrealistic timetables for programmes and weak controls, delays in delivery and wasted money. On the other hand, effective risk management has provided the means to develop successfully new services or new ways of working."

- The National Audit Office publication *Improving Public Services through Better Construction*, published in 2005, called for government departments to use the most appropriate contracting strategies which require "a well-developed capability to identify and manage the construction project risks".

- The 2005 Office of Government Commerce (OGC) report on UK construction in the public sector, entitled *Common Causes of Project Failure*, cited "Lack of skills and proven approach to project management and risk management" as one of eight causes of project failure.

- The National Audit Office publication *Ministry of Defence: Using the Contract to Maximise the Likelihood of Successful Project Outcomes*, published in June 2006, describes the Ministry of Defence's reforms to improve project performance. The Ministry has developed what it calls its gold standard criteria for achieving a successful contract. One of the criteria is called "negotiating from a common base" and states that an "enabler" for satisfying the criteria is "common analysis of the threats and opportunities undertaken early in the process by all parties with subsequent reviews".

- The 2007 Office of Government Commerce publication *Risk and Value Management* states that "poor risk management is known to be a major cause of project failure".

More and more professionals are appreciating the contribution of the discipline of risk management. Projects are growing in scale, complexity and value. For example, bridges and tunnels are getting longer, buildings taller, ports larger and the scale of information technology projects more ambitious. More importantly, project sponsors and stakeholders are becoming more demanding, more knowledgeable about risk management and less tolerant of excuses from experienced professionals who clearly "didn't see it coming" and appeared to be passive observers. When implemented effectively, risk management can deliver improved performance.

Clearly articulate the benefits of project risk management through the description of "value-add" examples.

7

Risk Resources

☑ **Risk team selection will directly influence risk management effectiveness**

I've always thought that recruiting is the heart and soul of what we do.
Steve Jobs, former CEO, Apple

Projects are a people business. They are delivered by people, not plans, processes or procedures. The implementation and execution of PRM is no exception. The quality of risk personnel will be critical to the delivery of effective risk management. Hence, spending time to very carefully select risk personnel is a wise investment. Leading organisations such as Apple and Microsoft have known for a long time that the calibre of their people has been fundamental to their success. While at the helm, Microsoft founder Bill Gates stated: "The key for us, number one, has always been hiring very smart people."

Job Description

A pre-requisite of the recruitment process is a job description. I continue to be surprised at how often scant attention is devoted to preparing a bespoke and most importantly a thoroughly considered job description. The job description must be a blend of many things. It must take into consideration the role context. Typically this entails thinking about the current composition of the team, succession planning, the duration of the project (if the organisation has been established for a single project), the culture of the organisation and any future workload. It also involves considering the risk management goals and process, the software currently in use, the current level of risk management maturity, the composition of the organisation and the project requirements. The project requirements might be the contract conditions of the delivery organisation which would describe the specific risk management activities to be completed. Job descriptions must make explicit the qualifications and experience required for the role, the specific capabilities necessary and any essential specialist skills (such as a second language). Job descriptions are a key communication tool to aid selection and inform candidates of the hiring organisation's requirements. Once shortlisting has been completed, the interview process can begin.

Software Competencies

Increasingly, there is a call for risk specialists to possess software competencies due to a growing number of projects choosing to implement quantitative risk analysis, commonly for cost and time. As costs are frequently time-related (and given the ability of planning tools to cost-load programmes), there is a call for risk personnel to have the ability to model time delays and the resultant cost ramifications. The capability to implement schedule risk analysis calls for knowledge of the use of programming software and schedule risk analysis software, as well as the principles of quantitative analysis. In particular, it calls for a specific understanding of how logic is included within schedules and how to include uncertainty within a schedule without disrupting the planned logic. The use by planners of interim milestones, constraints and alternative activity relationships necessitates careful consideration when studying the influence of threats and opportunities on outturn completion dates.

Industry Experience

Each industry has its own vocabulary, PLC, critical success factors, legislation, regulatory bodies and common sources of uncertainty. Hence, while there may be some similarities in project delivery between industries, for risk personnel to add value, they need to be familiar with the unique characteristics of the industry within which they work. The nuclear, oil and gas and rail industries, for instance, require knowledge of their specific gateway review process, terms and their definitions, project success factors and external approvals required.

Interview Process

At Apple, Steve Jobs involved several departments in the interview process and explained that:

Recruiting usually requires more than you alone can do, so I've found that collaborative recruiting and having a culture that recruits the 'A' players is the best way. Any interviewee will speak with at least a dozen people in several areas of this company, not just those in the area that he would work in. That way a lot of your "A" employees get broad exposure to the company and by having a company culture that supports them if they feel strongly enough, the current employees can veto a candidate.

Personality

However, not all recruitment processes are successful. Why do some appointments not work out? Many consultancies or contractors have hired employees who appeared to be just what they needed at the time of the interview, only to find out some time later that the person was far from appropriate. An ill-fitting recruit can result in a frustrating waste of time, effort and energy. In many instances it can also be an expensive mistake. Even worse than just a bad fit is a new recruit who is highly disruptive. Those who are uncooperative, disagreeable or argumentative can make life a misery. However, recruits that morph into being threatening or in extreme cases potentially violent are the most troublesome. So what goes wrong in a bad appointment? Are the individuals inexperienced? Is it insufficient industry exposure? Have they inadequate risk management skills or knowledge? The answer is most probably not. The problem usually involves personality. Undoubtedly, personality has a very important effect on performance of work, especially where the relationship with other team members will be crucial. What is personality and why is it important in the hiring process? Personality consists of core traits or temperaments that to a large extent determine how we behave. In other words, if you understand an individual's core personality, you will be able to predict with a reasonable degree of accuracy how that person will interact with people, carry out their job responsibilities, solve problems and handle setbacks and obstacles. So what are the common personality traits? The psychiatrist Karl Jung was content to divide personalities into extraverts and introverts, and Eysenck[1] subsequently regarded the factors of neuroticism and extroversion as being sufficient. The most extensive work was completed by Cattell,[2] who identified

---

1 Eysenck, H.J. and Eysenck, S.B.G. (1963) *The Eysenck Personality Inventory*. London: University of London Press.

2 Cattell, R.B. (1965) *The Scientific Analysis of Personality*. Harmondsworth: Penguin Books.

sixteen factors. Among them he identified: reserved/outgoing, affected by feelings/emotionally stable, submissive/dominant, tough minded/sensitive, group dependent/self-sufficient and trusting/suspicious. Subsequently, several independent sets of researchers identified five similar domains or dimensions of personality, called "the Big Five" factors, suitable for describing human personality. The theory based on the Big Five factors is called the Five Factor Model (FFM). The Big Five personality traits described by Costa and McCrae[3] emerged as a robust model for understanding the relationship between personality and various behaviours, and are as follows:

- *Openness to experience (inventive/curious vs. consistent/cautious).* This trait determines whether people are curious, likely to seek out new ideas and think creatively, or whether they are more conservative in outlook.

- *Conscientiousness (efficient/organised vs. easy-going/careless).* This trait determines our core method of working. At the one extreme, people are focused, organised, detail-oriented, perfectionistic and compulsive. At the opposite end, people tend to be flexible, spontaneous, tolerant of ambiguity and potentially disorganised.

- *Extraversion (outgoing/energetic vs. solitary/reserved).* This determines how naturally outgoing people are. Some people need a great deal of social interaction and seek stimulation in the company of others. Others need very little contact with people and may even be timid or a bit fearful of social encounters.

- *Agreeableness (friendly/compassionate vs. cold/unkind).* This trait involves how easy-going and tolerant as opposed to how intense and potentially irritable a person behaves. The extremes are those who go through life in a fairly calm fashion and at the other extreme those who get frustrated frequently. Easy-going people may be easy to get along with, but may also lack drive and determination. Intense and irritable people may be highly driven and goal-oriented, but may also ruffle feathers.

3   Costa, P.T., Jr. and McCrae, R.R. (1992). *Revised NEO Personality Inventory (NEO-PI-R) and NEO Five-Factor Inventory (NEO-FFI) Manual.* Odessa, FL: Psychological Assessment Resources.

- *Neuroticism (sensitive/nervous vs. secure/confident)*. This trait refers to emotional well-being and people's degree of self-confidence. It refers to the tendency to experience unpleasant emotions easily, such as anger, anxiety, depression or vulnerability. Some people show emotions readily and others are "stony-faced" and rarely change their expression. In addition, there are people who are predisposed to emotional outbursts or even violent behaviour.

In the hiring process, there are two primary uses of personality assessment. First, the most basic personality assessment is used to screen out potential problem employees. This type of assessment relates mostly to the "emotional well-being" aspect of the Big Five dimensions. While predicting these types of problem traits is not an exact science, it is argued that screening for the potential for these problems to occur can be done accurately and reliably. Once potential "bad" traits have been screened out, the second use of personality assessment involves gauging the fit between an individual and the specific requirements of the job and the organisational culture. So, how can you hedge your bets that you do not hire problem employees or employees that do not fit the requirements of the job or the culture of your company? In addition to multiple interviews and good interviewing techniques, psychological assessment may help.

Psychological assessment (also commonly referred to as testing and profiling) is now very popular with companies in the UK and the US. It is reported that 40 per cent of large companies in the US use psychological assessment to screen candidates prior to hiring. As such, it is very big business. The catalysts for these tests are employers' previous bad experiences, the cost of hiring and training employees, and the need to make more informed decisions. Employers want to judge as best they can that potential employees are suitable before hiring them. In the US, the most frequent reason given by employers for increasing testing is the need to have a selection process which can withstand legal challenges. Many companies consult outside companies to give and assess these tests in an effort to keep the tests unbiased. Psychological assessments typically examine the following: general intellectual level and problem solving, emotional maturity and personality, management style, decision making and organisational skills, leadership competencies, ambition and aspirations. There are currently well over 2,500 personality questionnaires on the market and each year dozens of new companies appear with their own "new" products. Some of these products are broad-based tests designed to classify basic personality types, while others are designed to test candidates for their suitability for a particular job. While many of the well-established companies who provide personality tests strive to operate to the highest ethical and professional standards, with such a growth in the industry (combined with low barriers to entry and little official regulation), it is inevitable that it has attracted entrants with varying degrees of competence and integrity. This situation is made more difficult since most of the companies that produce personality tests are very secretive about their methodologies and refuse to make public crucial information about how their tests were developed or how well they work, claiming that this information is "proprietary". There is a historical association with academic and occupational psychology which gives the personality testing industry a degree of credibility that some claim it does not always deserve. The usefulness and accuracy of even the most well-established tests, which have been the subject of hundreds of research papers, remain highly controversial among psychologists. The most advisable way to find a consultancy offering psychological tests in the UK is through the British Psychological Society (http://www.bps.org.uk), in Australia through the Australian Psychological Society (http://www.psychology.org.au) and in the US through the American Psychological Association (http://www.apa.org/science/programs/testing/index.aspx).

Composition of the risk team is critical to the effectiveness of PRM.

☑ The budget will dictate the level of risk management support

Goals should drive budgets, budgets should not determine goals.
Robbins, S. and Coulter, M. (2012)
Management, Global Edition, *11th edn. Harlow: Pearson Education*

As with any project discipline, the resources assigned to the delivery of that discipline will have a direct bearing on the level and quality of the service provided. The discipline of PRM is no different. The budget for PRM will have a direct bearing on the level of provision of risk management support that may be provided. However, from experience, frequently there is a misalignment, sometimes of a substantial nature, between the expectations of the recipient of risk management services and the budget allocated to risk services. This can be the result of the individual (or individuals) preparing the resource provision for risk management: not being an experienced project professional (and not being conversant with the time required to complete activities), being a project professional but not consulting a risk practitioner, consulting but not accepting the recommendations of a risk practitioner, using heuristics rather than preparing a bottom-up cost breakdown or electing to suppress the costs for commercial advantage – accepting the required scope of service will be a challenge to satisfy or may not be met. When developing the budget for PRM, consideration needs to be given to the recruitment costs, staffing costs (including pay rises, insurance and bonuses), travel costs, expenses, staff contingency, office space costs, hardware, software, staff training, project team training and staff development costs:

- *Recruitment costs*: recruitment costs should be factored into the budget regardless of whether the organisation does not normally tend to use recruiting organisations in order to cover the event where using recruiters cannot be avoided. The costs should reflect the current market rates, which may change over time due to low demand or buoyancy in the market.

- *Staffing*: careful consideration needs to be given to the calculation of the staff costs. This will entail considering the number and grade of staff required, their duration on the project, salaries, benefits, insurance, pay rises and possible bonuses. Consideration needs to be given to the most appropriate point in time when staff are taken off the project. It may be prudent to retain staff to cover the transition from project execution to operations in order to address any movement in risk ownership to the operator.

- *Travel*: the budget should make provision for travel costs to cover attendance at meetings, presentations, workshops, audits, training, team-building sessions, conferences, milestone progress functions and similar activities.

- *Expenses*: expenses typically cover subsistence costs, such as accommodation and meals relating to trips taken away from the office.

- *Staffing contingency*: as with all budgets, it is always prudent to include a contingency. If staff leave, unplanned expenditure may occur/be required to cover recruitment costs and/or short-term consultancy or staff support.

- *Office space*: officie space is typically calculated as a function of the number of personnel, the floor space allocated to each grade of personnel and the cost per unit of floor space populated by the risk team/department.

- *Hardware*: the hardware will depend on the size of the organisation (the number of personnel), the use of a web-based risk database, the use of a Microsoft SQL server, the number of database users and the need for a Local Area Network (LAN) and a Wide Area Network (WAN).

- *Software*: software costs can be considerable if the decision is taken to purchase a web-based risk database (and the cost is based on the number of licences), project planning tools, quantitative risk analysis modelling software and graphics software, as well as word processing and spreadsheet software.

- *Training of risk personnel*: staff training needs will vary considerably between individuals based on their experience. Training may be required for rudimentary or advanced risk management practices and techniques, workshop facilitation, the use of a database, the application of sophisticated software planning tools, statistical analysis, use of quantitative analysis software tools, aspects of project, change, stakeholder or value management, spreadsheet modelling, presentations, in-house software, document control software and so on.

- *Training of project staff by risk personnel*: it is common for projects to provide PRM training for their project personnel to ensure that personnel are all at the same level in terms of awareness and project requirements. The training may include the objectives and benefits of risk management, the background to PRM, risk management terms and their definition, the risk documents and their purpose, the risk process, integration between risk management and other disciplines, risk reporting requirements and risk KPIs.

- *Staff development costs (courses/conferences)*: in recognition of the need to support and carry out staff development in order to retain and develop team members, it may be appropriate to sponsor attendance at risk or risk-related courses or conferences, depending on their relevance to the project or the organisation.

The budget is a primary "building block" necessary to create a stable foundation for effective risk management.

8

Systems

☑ **A risk management framework must establish a firm foundation**

Uncertainty is the worst of all evils until the moment when reality makes us regret uncertainty.

Alphonse Karr, French journalist and author

The effectiveness of the discipline of risk management (like the other project management Knowledge Areas)[1] will be determined predominantly by the way in which it has been established. The International Standard ISO 31000 recommends that the implementation of risk management is supported by a framework. For ease of assimilation, the definition[2] of a framework and its purpose, endorsement and contribution are described in summary in Table 8.1 below.

A framework is the highest structure in the architecture of risk management. A framework supports the creation of foundations and organisational arrangements for embedding risk management. These foundations may be described as a series of building blocks which collectively underpin the delivery of risk management. They will be composed of, for instance, the objectives, management commitment to risk management, budget, personnel, processes, procedures, hardware and software. However, these building blocks must be in balance. There must be an equal focus on both the "hard" aspects of risk management (i.e. the processes and procedures) and the "soft" aspects (i.e. personnel, norms and behaviours). For example, a project may have highly sophisticated risk processes to manage risks; however, unless these processes are supported by management and staff with the appropriate competencies, aptitude and mindset, the framework will most likely be ineffective.

---

1   "Knowledge Areas" are the project disciplines described within the Project Management Institute's *A Guide to the Project Management Body of Knowledge (PMBOK Guide)*, 4th edn.
2   The definition is based on the definition included within ISO Guide 73:2009, "Risk Management – Vocabulary".

Table 8.1   Risk management framework

What is a framework?	In summary, a framework is a set of components that together provide a structure for designing, implementing, monitoring, reviewing and continually improving risk management throughout the project. (Definition adapted from *ISO Guide* 73: 2009.)
What is its purpose?	Put simply, the purpose of establishing a risk management framework is to ensure that risks are effectively identified and responded to in a manner that is appropriate to the context of the project, its ability to manage risks, the risk management resources and the receptiveness of the project to the discipline of risk management.
Who will endorse it?	It must be read and endorsed by those accountable for risk management on the project.
Will it contribute to the success of a project?	The Standard is predicated on the belief that risk management will, among other things, "improve corporate governance", "establish a reliable basis for decision making and planning", "encourage proactive rather than reactive management" and "improve operational effectiveness and efficiency". Hence a framework will contribute to project success if it improves the opportunity for risk management to succeed.
What will it provide?	The Standard states the framework will provide "the foundations and organisational arrangements that will embed it [risk management] throughout the organisation at all levels".

The Standard describes establishing a mandate and commitment for risk management, followed by four incremental steps which have been abbreviated here to "Design framework", "Implement framework", "Monitor framework" and "Improve framework". These steps are depicted as a continuous improvement cycle (see Figure 8.1 below), whereby the use of the framework informs opportunities for improvement. Each step in turn seeks to initially support and then improve on the inculcating of risk into the day-to-day activities of the project.

Mandate and commitment: the mandate for PRM is derived from the Project Director and/or Project Board and is issued in order to support successful project delivery. The continuous engagement by and support of the senior leadership team is critical. Without it, risk management will fail. In addition, it must be fully embraced by the contracting parties who are directly responsible for the delivery of the project (i.e. consultants, contractors, subcontractors and major suppliers). To this end, projects must ensure that the contract clauses (which stipulate the completion of specified risk management responsibilities) are adequately satisfied. The Project Director (and Board) must lead the commitment to risk management by implementing the actions described in Figure 8.2.

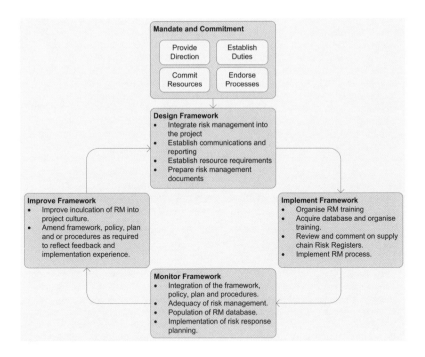

Figure 8.1   Components of a project risk framework

Note: "RM" is the acronym for risk management.

Futhermore, the senior leadership team in particular must lead the commitment to risk management by accepting and recognising the discipline of risk management as a "value-add" discipline where time invested in it will directly contribute to a successful outcome and satisfaction of the project objectives.

Design framework: this is the first step in the continuous improvement cycle illustrated above. The "design framework" step is described in Figure 8.3 as having four primary elements which have been labelled "Integration", "Communication and reporting", "Resources" and "Documents". These elements describe the *where*, to *whom*, *what resources* and *which documents*, respectively. In other words, *where* will risk management be incorporated within the project processes, to *whom* will risk reports be issued, *what organisation* will be established to deliver risk management and *which documents* will be prepared to convey risk management intentions?

Integration (stage gate reviews): as referred to under "Integration" (within the "Design Framework" step), the design of the framework must reflect the stage gate reviews (see Figure 8.4) that will be undertaken.

Provide Direction
- Align risk management with the business case and project objectives.
- Ensure risk management is integrated with the other project disciplines.
- Communicate the benefits of risk management to stakeholders.
- Establish internal and external communication and reporting requirements.

Establish Duties
- Define accountability for risk management on the project.
- Identify the responsibilities of the Risk Manager (or equivalent).
- Include risk management responsibilities within senior staff contracts and job descriptions.
- Identify risk champions within the project disciplines.

Commit Resources
- Allocate an appropriate budget which reflects the planned implementation rather than being based on some simple heuristic.
- Allocate an adequate number of qualified, experienced and motivated personnel.
- Provide funding for risk a database, appropriate number of licenses, hosting, manuals, annual support and training.
- Provide adequate office facilities.

Endorse Processes
- Endorse proposed compliance with legislation and regulations.
- Endorse risk management being critical to decision making.
- Endorse the adoption of international risk management standards.
- Accept proposed risk management key performance indicators.
- Endorse the project documents - such as the policy, plan and supporting procedures making compliance mandatory rather than discretionary.

Figure 8.2   Mandate and commitment

Integration
- Integrate risk management across the project life-cycle.
- Incorporate risk management within the stage gate review process.
- Inculcate risk management within decision making and project wide change management.
- Reflect the internal and external environment (the context) within the approach adopted for risk management.

Communication and Reporting
- Determine method for establishing, recording, debating, aligning and disseminating the stakeholder's requirements/interests.
- Establish internal reporting to aid decision making.
- Establish external reporting to satisfy sponsor and other stakeholder requirements.
- Develop an internal and external communication plan.

Resources
- Define the risk management resource requirements and prepare an organisational structure which reflects the needs and the available budget.
- Define the number of risk positions and the requirements of each position.
- Establish risk hardware and software requirements.

Documents
- Prepare the risk management policy which sets out the project's commitment to and rationale for managing risk.
- Prepare the risk management plan based on the adopted standards.
- Prepare the procedures and practice notes designed to support the implementation of the plan.

Figure 8.3   Design framework

In summary stage gate reviews are decision gates which occur at the end of intermediate project stages to determine if a project should proceed to the next stage. These reviews are a "peer review" carried out by an independent individual or team from outside the project who use their knowledge and experience to examine the progress to date and the likelihood of the project being successful. The review uses detailed desk top studies of the existing project information and a series of interviews with the project team. It uses the review team's experience to provide a valuable additional perspective on the issues facing the project team and provides an external challenge as to whether the current phase has been completed or not. Critically, it will recommend whether the project should move on to the next project phase or not and hence whether further funds should be committed to the project. The framework should describe which reviews will be undertaken and the composition of each review stage. An example of where the absence of stage gate reviews led to detrimental consequences is the Millennium Train Project described in Case Study 21 below. The absence of reviews deprived the project of the ability to articulate (and subsequently manage) the risk exposure and impose more control to reduce cost increases and schedule delays.

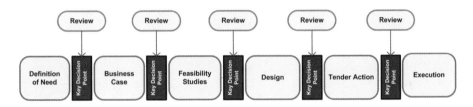

Figure 8.4   Project life cycle

Figure 8.4 illustrates a simplified PLC for illustrative purposes only. Clearly, there are very many permutations on the project stages that may be adopted and the sequence in which they are implemented. However, the principle remains that a project's risk exposure should be re-examined prior to the next project stage in order to gain an understanding of the degree of the current risk exposure and the uncertainty associated with, for instance, the completion date and the cost of the project.

The Gateway Unit of the State Government of Victoria, Australia,[3] implemented a Gateway Review Process (GRP) based on the UK's Office of

3   http://www.gatewayreview.dtf.vic.gov.au.

Government Commerce's Gateway™ Process. It was first introduced to Victoria in 2003. The GRP has been made mandatory for what it terms as high-value and/or high-risk (HV/HR) projects. HV/HR projects are defined as all projects with a total estimated investment (TEI) of more than $100 million (regardless of funding source) and/or projects identified as high risk. Analysis of Gateway Review findings (of over 150 reviews) by the Unit consistently identifies inadequate risk management as a reason behind limited project/programme success. As part of the review of the risk management process, it asks "are there sufficient resources to ensure that risk management processes are in place and sustainable?", recognising that both the initial and the ongoing levels of risk resources will be critical to effective risk management.

CASE STUDY 21 – THE MILLENNIUM TRAIN PROJECT, AUSTRALIA[1]

The Millennium Train Project was initiated on 8 October 1998 when the New South Wales State Rail Authority (StateRail) signed a contract for the design, building and 15 years of maintenance of 81 new suburban double-decker electric passenger cars. As a consequence of the combination of the technical complexity of the project and the lack of appeal of the contract to international bidders, the very limited number of suitable contractors resulted in a weak bargaining position for StateRail. A key finding of the project review was that at the time of consideration of the contract, key decision makers on the StateRail Board and the Minister for Transport had not been provided with a risk management plan for the project. It later transpired that despite the Millennium Train Project's contractual provisions, when significant risks materialised, they were borne disproportionately by StateRail. The New South Wales Auditor-General found that the project came in well beyond schedule and considerably over-budget. By June 2003, capital costs had increased by $114 million (or 24 per cent) to $588 million, and total project costs had increased by $98.4 million (or 17 per cent) to $658 million. The audit recommended that: internal audit function should be involved at crucial stages of major projects and in ongoing risk management reviews; future projects should review the adequacy of liquidated damages clauses included within contracts and specifically how and when liquidated damages would be applied in the event of poor contractor performance; and there should be more careful assessment of the options for responding to risks, as contractual provisions do not necessarily avoid or mitigate risk events to business objectives.

---

1   Auditor General (2003) "Performance Audit – State Rail Authority – The Millennium Train Project". The Audit Office of New South Wales.

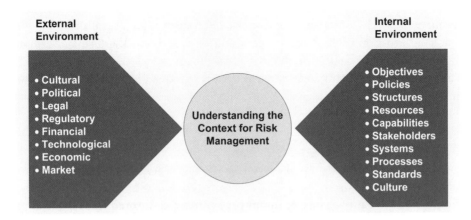

**External
Environment**

**Internal
Environment**

• Cultural
• Political
• Legal
• Regulatory
• Financial
• Technological
• Economic
• Market

Understanding the
Context for Risk
Management

• Objectives
• Policies
• Structures
• Resources
• Capabilities
• Stakeholders
• Systems
• Processes
• Standards
• Culture

Figure 8.5   Context for risk management based on ISO 31000

Integration (context): as referred to under "Integration" (within the "Design framework" step), the design of the framework must reflect and be tailored to both the internal and external contexts of the project. For those familiar with implementing project and risk management, it will be a memorable fact that no two projects are identical. The environment within which a project operates has the potential to significantly impact its ability to achieve its objectives. To fully understand the risk exposure of the project, a thorough knowledge of the organisation of the project and the internal and external environment in which it operates is required. Figure 8.5 summarises the external and internal factors described in ISO 31000 which shape a project's setting or context and which will impinge on the ease with which effective risk management can be implemented.

Resources: what can be accomplished with risk management will be directly related to the size and competency of the risk team, the stage of the project at which risk personnel are introduced to the project, the degree of freedom they have to engage with the project team, the extent to which they are kept aware of developments on the project, the software tools made available to them and the manner in which they are involved in decision making. Resources include assets, people, finance, information and eventually time.

Documents: these are the means by which the project's intent and the chosen method of managing risk are communicated to the risk team, the project team members and the stakeholders inside and outside of the project. They should reflect the project's current and targeted maturity level, the risk management resources, the PLC, planned contractual relationships to secure delivery, the risk standard upon which the process will be based and the terms and their definition that will be used so that the project team "speak the same language". The sequence in which the documents are prepared is illustrated in Figure 8.6 below.

Figure 8.6   Sequence of document preparation as defined in ISO 31000

Implement framework: implementing the framework requires preparing and disseminating a number of interrelated documents to describe how risk management is to be implemented across the project (including where appropriate the use of risk software tools). The numbering adopted below corresponds with the numbering within Figure 8.7:

1.   The agreement with the sponsor informs the risk framework (the sponsor is defined in this instance as the individual or organisation that is providing the funding, stipulating the objectives and clarifying the definition of need).

2.   The Project Execution Plan sets out in a comprehensive way the way in which the project is to be executed, including the implementation of risk management.

3.   The framework is implemented as a sequence of activities which are revisited as part of an iterative cycle of design, implement, monitor and improve (similar to the "plan-do-check-act" cycle adopted by business continuity and other disciplines).

4.   The framework in turn informs the risk policy, which in summary is a statement of intent and is endorsed by the Project Director and the senior leadership team.

5.   Subservient to the Policy is the Risk Management Plan, which describes in detail the "what, who, when and how" of risk management implementation.

6.   Subservient to and a component of the Risk Management Plan is the Risk Management Process, which describes the individual (but interdependent) steps within the process.

7.   The implementation of risk management is supported by a database when present.

8.   When the process is being implemented and the database is being populated, it is then possible to report on the degree of exposure to threats and the opportunities that may be potentially exploited.

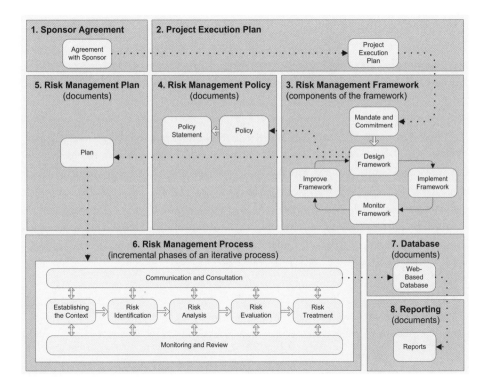

Figure 8.7   Implement framework

Monitor framework: in order to ensure that risk management is effective and continues to support a project's performance (measured in terms of adhering to the project's objectives), the project should: ensure the risk management framework, policy, plan and procedures are integrated and aligned; report on the adequacy of risk management in terms of the identified risks, response planning (including the specific actions described to address the individual risks) and the movement in risk exposure; ensure that the database is being populated appropriately and regularly updated, and report on any changes required in the approach being adopted for risk management in order to overcome instances where implementation is less than satisfactory.

Improve framework: based on the findings of the "Monitor framework" step, a project should seek to improve the inculcation of risk management into decision making, the PLC, the gate review process and the project supply chain down into the project's day-to-day activities. As a consequence of any agreed changes to the risk management practices, it may be necessary to amend the framework, policy and/or plan.

Recording and communicating the framework: while ISO 31000 describes a framework as a set of components rather than as a stand-alone document, many organisations have found it necessary to prepare a framework to communicate their risk management intentions. This provides a vehicle for recording which documents have been prepared, their purpose and the relationship between them – in other words, how the parts of the jigsaw fit together. This is particularly important when separate risk documents are prepared by organisations for their corporation as a whole and for programmes they undertake, and the individual projects that make up these programmes.

The usefulness of a risk management framework hinges on acceptance by senior management of the need for the "building blocks" described within it.

☑ Commitment commences with a risk policy

> *Individual commitment to a group effort – that is what makes a team*
> *work, a company work, a society work, a civilization work.*
>
> *Vince Lombardi, American football coach who led the*
> *Green Bay Packers to five NFL championships*

What is the true purpose of a risk policy? Why go to the trouble of preparing one? What is it that you want to accomplish? Reflecting on the meaning given in the *Oxford Everyday Dictionary*, a policy (in general terms) can be considered simply as a "statement of intent". A risk policy could be defined as no more than a declaration to implement risk management. Clearly, it is more than that. As described by British Standard 31100, a policy "should set the direction, scope and objectives for risk management, and take into consideration the context, key stakeholders and the organisation's existing risk management capability and maturity". However, as described in the ISO 31000 Standard, the risk management policy should clearly state the organisation's objectives for risk management while at the same time describing: the organisation's rationale for managing risk; the links between the organisation's objectives and the risk policy; the accountabilities and responsibilities for managing risk; the method of resolution of conflicting interests; the way in which risk performance will be measured and reported; the commitment to make the necessary resources available to assist those accountable and responsible for managing risk; and the commitment to review and improve the risk management policy and framework periodically and in response to an event or change in circumstances. Therefore, a risk policy is predominantly (but not exclusively) a "commitment" to risk management. As any risk manager/ coordinator will tell you, securing and communicating the commitment of senior management to risk management is a cornerstone of inculcating risk management within a project organisation and the project's supply chain. It is important to be able to tie senior management to the implementation of risk management and to communicate to the project team as a whole that the discipline has the support of the project leadership. Without the confirmed commitment of the Project Director and the senior management team, the value of a policy and the effectiveness of risk management as a whole will be severely diminished. This commitment needs to be clearly articulated in the policy. Ultimately, there needs to be commitment to and engagement in risk management by the complete project team. I believe Vince Lombardi clearly understood that, in order to achieve success, individual team members have to be committed to and work towards the common goal. One possible way to structure this commitment within a risk policy is with the aid of a series of questions, the "Five Ws" (and one H), once captured by Rudyard Kipling in his *Just So Stories*, first published in 1902.[4] A more contemporary perspective on the six questions is the list proposed by Chapman and Ward[5] included in Table 8.2, although not specifically identified to structure a risk policy.

Table 8.2   Chapman and Ward: six basic questions

1	who	Who are the parties that are ultimately involved?	(parties)
2	why	What do the parties want to achieve?	(motives)
3	what	What is it that the parties are interested in?	(design)
4	whichway	How is it to be done?	(activities)
5	wherewithal	What resources are required?	(resources)
6	when	When does it have to be done?	(project timetable)

The risk management policy may include commitments to:

- make explicit on behalf of whom the risk management will be conducted, the parties involved in the project, the nature of the relationship between them and the source of risk they may generate. Understanding on whose behalf the risk management practices will be conducted will assist in determining the risk reporting requirements, which will feed forward into how risk management is to be implemented to gather the required information. Reporting can absorb a considerable amount of time and if the reporting requirements are substantially different between stakeholders, this may need to be reflected in the budget (*who*);

- adopt the discipline of risk management to assist in securing the project objectives (in accordance with any declared priority and

---

4   At the end of Kipling's story called "The Elephant's Child", he includes a poem which begins as follows:
"I keep six honest serving-men, (They taught me all I knew); Their names are What and Why and When, and How and Where and Who." The "Five Ws and One H" were once adopted as a problem-solving method and were referred to as the "Kipling Method" as a consequence of the poem. They were used to explore problems by challenging them with these questions.
5   Chapman, C. and Ward, S. (2003) *Project Risk Management: Processes, Techniques and Insights*, 2nd edn. Chichester: John Wiley & Sons.

the organisation's risk appetite/aversion), recognising that risk management is a core project management capability, and also to continuously record and analyse those risks which may adversely affect or enhance the business case (*why*);

- apply risk management to the project activities, which may be described as the overall stages in a PLC, commencing with the business case, following through to a project activity schedule/plan as the project becomes defined and culminating with the handover to the end users/operator. Commitments to ensure that there is sufficient focus and attention at the very early stages of a project when there is the greatest uncertainty and when risk management can make the largest contribution may also be included (*what*);

- make explicit those accountable and responsible for risk management and make resources available to them, whether this be in the form of a budget, staff, training, specialist software or databases, in a timely manner (*wherewithal*);

- undertake risk management continuously with a specific focus at critical decision points during the PLC, such as stage gates (*when*);

- implement a consistent process (together with methods and tools) to manage risk (reflecting the current and planned risk maturity levels), communicate the risk terms and definitions (so that there is a common language), report on the output of the risk management process (describing the required format, content and timing), describe the way in which risk performance will be measured, conduct periodic reviews of the framework, policy plan, procedures and software, and manage the risks according to the confidentiality, integrity and availability of the project information (*whichway*).

Figure 8.8 below summarises key commitments required from a project's senior management to support the delivery of effective PRM. Risk management cannot be driven from the "bottom up" of an organisation, but only from the "top down". Hence, it must have the visible commitment of the project's leadership.

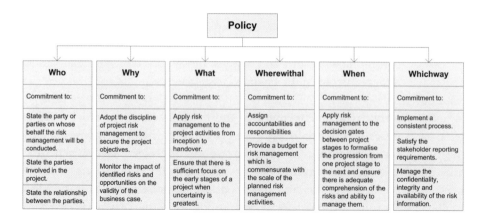

Figure 8.8   Aspects of the commitment to risk management recorded in a project risk policy

> A key function of a risk policy is to secure, record and disseminate senior management commitment to risk management in order to assist in inculcating risk management within a project.

☑ Effective decision making is dependent on risk management

> *Decision making is not a mechanical job. It is risk-taking and a challenge to judgement.*
>
> Peter F. Drucker, *management consultant and author*

When pursuing growth, regardless of a business's strategy, it has to decide what opportunities it wants to pursue and the level of risk it is willing to accept. Hence, value and risk cannot be meaningfully separated.[6] The business activity selected to support the strategy, commonly in the form of a project, should be chosen on the basis of maximising opportunities while at the same time minimising risks. As such, threat and opportunity management must receive equal attention and it is important for boards to choose the right balance. This is succinctly expressed by the National Audit Office, which states that: "a business risk management approach offers the possibility for

---

6   Ristuccia, H. (2013) "10 Skills for Making Risk-Intelligent Decisions", *CFO Journal*, 11 January. At the time of writing, Henry Ristuccia is a partner with Deloitte & Touche LLP.

striking a judicious and systematically[7] argued balance between [downside] risk and opportunity in the form of the contradictory pressures for greater entrepreneurialism on the one hand and limitation of downside risks on the other".[8] What opportunities are available should emerge from the analysis of potential growth strategies. To pursue any opportunity requires a business to make a decision. Given the axiom that risk management is integral to effective decision making,[9] project risk practitioners need to understand the anatomy of decision making in order to ensure that inherent risk (composed of threats and opportunities) is adequately articulated. When margins diminish, as they have done after the credit crisis, attention to risk exposure has to be more vigilant. This opinion is echoed by Mike Elliot (global mining and metals leader for Ernst & Young) in the following statement: "The bottom line is that if returns start to wane, then there is a greater imperative for organizations to tightly and more effectively manage their risks to maintain an adequate risk/reward balance."[10]

The Structure of Decision Making

Decision making (which is also described in the literature as problem solving) requires a structured approach and is a process that needs to be managed. There are many examples of approaches to decision making. The structured approach illustrated in Figure 8.9 is typical. The steps in the process are discussed in turn below.

---

7   A principle contained within ISO 31000 is that "Risk management is systematic, structured and timely".
8   National Audit Office (2000) *Supporting Innovation: Managing Risk in Government Departments*, report by the Comptroller and Auditor General, 17 August. London: The Stationery Office.
9   See principle c) within ISO 31000 (Risk management – principles and guidelines), which states that "Risk management is part of decision making".
10 Ernst & Young "Business Risks Facing Mining and Minerals, 2012–2013", available at: http://www.ey.com/Publication/vwLUAssets/Business-risk-facing-mining-and-metals-2012-2013/$FILE/Business-risk-facing-mining-and-metals-2012-2013.pdf.

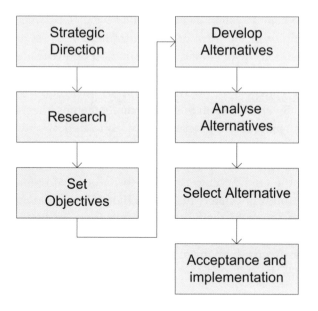

Figure 8.9   Structured approach to decision making

Strategic Direction

Any organisation has to decide how it might develop in the future in order to exploit identified strengths and opportunities. Peter Drucker[11] identified as far back as the 1960s that risk exposure increases as the scale of opportunity increases. He describes three primary types of opportunities. They are labelled *additive, complementary* and *breakthrough*. He explains that *additive opportunities* more fully exploit existing resources, where the risks should be small as the returns are always limited. As a consequence, *additive opportunities* are rarely treated as high-priority efforts and typically are not allowed to take resources away from *complementary* or *breakthrough* opportunities. A *complementary opportunity* is described as one that offers something new, will always require at least one new knowledge area in which excellence has to be attained and will require a change to the structure of the business. A *complementary opportunity* always carries with it considerable risk. Drucker describes a *breakthrough opportunity* as one that requires great effort, the employment of first-class resources and commonly considerable capital investment. The risk is always great. Such an opportunity changes the fundamental economic characteristics and capacity of a business.

---

11 Drucker, P.F. (1967) *Managing for Results*. London: Pan Books.

Examples of these categories are as follows:

- Additive strategies are based on finding new markets for existing products.

- Complementary strategies can include creating similar products to those currently manufactured, but with new materials and offering them in existing markets. Examples include the car manufacturers Ford and General Motors lending money to car buyers.

- Breakthrough strategies are based on diversifying and launching new products into new markets. It is the most risky option of the three. Examples include the Sony Walkman and IKEA flat-pack furniture.

Research

Decisions based on poor information can lead to the squandering of an opportunity, accepting unnecessary risks, misallocating resources and ultimately not achieving the business' strategic objectives. Any decision-making process is likely to be enhanced by the use of reliable and relevant information based on the best current evidence from similar projects. That is the premise behind evidence-based management (EBMgt) proposed by the researchers Pfeffer and Sutton,[12] which is the systematic use of the best available evidence to improve management practice.[13] The four essential elements[14] of EBMgt are the decision maker's expertise and judgement; external evidence that has been evaluated by the decision maker; the opinions, preferences and values of those who have a stake in the decision; and the relevant internal organisational factors, such as context, circumstances and personnel.

Robust research is dependent on the development of both a research methodology for data collection and a timeline to avoid the situation where the data is only available when the opportunity has passed. The research method must be both reliable and valid. Reliable here means that should the research be repeated, the results would be the same, and valid refers to the data being current, accurate, complete, derived from source and unambiguous.

12 Pfeffer, J. and Sutton, R.I. (2006), "Evidence-Based Management", *Harvard Business Review*, January.
13 Reay, T., Berta, W. and Kohn, M.K. (2009) "What's the Evidence on Evidence-Based Management?", *Academy of Management Perspectives*, November, 5.
14 Robbins, S.P. and Coulter, M. (2012) *Management*, 11th edn. Harlow: Pearson Education.

Set Project Objectives

The project objectives need to be selected with extreme care and stated unambiguously. This will enable appropriate alternative options to be identified and evaluated. The project objectives will reflect and be a subset of the organisation's objectives. Targets can be established which are interim objectives to be accomplished prior to the realisation of the overall objectives. These targets need to be Specific, Measurable, Achievable, Relevant and Timebound (SMART). When setting objectives, it is helpful to consider a series of questions such as:

- What would success look like?

- How would success be measured?

- What aspects of the project would be critical to success?

- Can the objectives and targets be established in such a way that progress towards meeting them could be assessed?

Develop Alternative Options

A subrule is that effective decisions are those that have considered a range of alternative options which satisfy the strategic direction that the organisation wishes to follow. The available options that a business may pursue include the following, which would ultimately translate into projects, but none is risk-free:

- *Internal development (often referred to as organic growth)*: this is where the organisation uses its own internal capabilities and resources to pursue its chosen strategy. It is considered to offer a lower risk, but the speed of growth is likely to be slow.

- *Takeovers/acquisitions or mergers*: this option affords the opportunity to acquire resources, knowledge of a particular product and its market, and/or a new product range. An example of an unsuccessful acquisition is when Hewlett-Packard (HP) acquired Compaq. Prior to the acquisition, HP did not conduct any research into how customers viewed Compaq products. By the time HP discovered that customers perceived Compaq products as inferior, it was too late and HP's performance suffered. As a consequence, the CEO of HP, Carly Fiorina, lost her job.

- *Strategic alliances*: this route may support gaining access to technology or new markets. Examples of two failed alliances for Cisco, as identified by Greg Fox (Cisco's Marketing Director of Strategic Alliances)[15] were with Motorola and Ericsson (who had turned into competitors as a result of acquisitions).

In a perverse way, threats indicate where to look for opportunities. Drucker considers that converting threats into opportunities can bring extraordinary returns. He considers three questions that will bring out the hidden potential of a business:

- What are the constraints and limitations that make the business vulnerable, impede its effectiveness and hold down its economic results?

- What are the imbalances of the business?

- What are we afraid of, what do we see as a threat to this business and how can we use it as an opportunity?

Consideration of vulnerability or restraint as an opportunity may involve examination of the manufacturing process, the economics of the industry and the economics of the market. Reviewing chronic imbalances (weaknesses) and turning them into opportunities may involve examination of the level of management and marketing, together with the planned level of investment in research and development, which may be uncoordinated with production.

Early on, it is important to consult widely to develop a meaningful set of options to aid in the selection of the optimum solution.[16] Each option will have a different risk profile (degree of risk exposure).

For option definition, it is often necessary to construct a model (in the form of a spreadsheet) of the option to facilitate its evaluation. A model is a representation of a real situation. Those models which reflect the uncertainty of

---

15 Arndt, M. (2009) "Cisco's Failures in Corporate Alliances", *Bloomberg Businessweek*, 4 December.

16 If the project is to obtain larger premises, for instance, consideration might be given to renting, building new premises, purchasing existing premises, refurbishing existing premises, refurbishing purchased accommodation, occupying multiple sites, relocating to another part of the country or another country, outsourcing non-critical functions to reduce or remove the need for more floor space or sharing premises with a trading partner.

the inputs are referred to as stochastic. This uncertainty is typically represented by the significant uncertainties (threats and opportunities) and the relationship between them. In addition, the model must be accompanied by an explanation of any assumptions made. It should be recognised that the quality of models can be detrimentally affected by a number of issues, some of which are listed below:

- No forecasting model can be 100 per cent reliable.

- The less known and understood about the project, the less effective the forecasting will be.

- The experience and ability of the individual or individuals constructing the model.

- The model may contain errors, such as incorrect formulas, which collect information from the wrong cells.

- The selection of the probabilities for the uncertainties may be inappropriate and may not reflect reality.

- The risk identification process may be superficial and may not examine the whole PLC, risks that may emanate from all of the project disciplines or all of the primary stakeholders.

- The relationship between the uncertainties has not been modelled.

- Facts have been concealed from those constructing the model.

- The potential fluctuation in material or component prices is not modelled.

- It will not be possible to model the unknown unknowns. Risk management is concerned with known unknowns.

Alternative Analysis

A facet of option review is to make sure that the project stakeholders who will have to do something to make the decision effective (or who could strive to sabotage it) have been forced to participate openly and responsibly in the appraisal process.

During option reviews, decision makers need to remain open-minded. Effective decision makers will know from experience that there are those who are ill-informed, who are consumed by their own self-interest, who lack adequate comprehension of the subject or who are just plain mischief-makers. However, they do not assume that if a person disagrees with their proposed option (which they themselves see as clear and obvious), they automatically fall into one of these camps. They know that unless proven otherwise, the dissenter must be considered as both knowledgeable and fair-minded. Therefore, it has to be assumed that he or she has reached his or her viewpoint based on a different perspective. The effective manager must then ask what is this person aware of that would make an alternative view appear so rational and appropriate. Hence, the effective manager has to be concerned with understanding the rationale behind why dissent may have arisen.

A subrule is that this understanding will come from *critical thinking*. *Critical thinking* may be defined as "the skilled and active evaluation (by metacognition) of a belief (and the reasoning offered to support it), through the knowledgeable application of methods of logical enquiry and reasoning". The word "critical" as used in the expression "critical thinking" does not mean disapproval or negativity. The word "evaluation" is included as this is the process of determining the merit, quality, worth or value of an option. The term "metacognition" is used to describe the process that individuals undertake to think about their own thinking. The word "belief" is used to represent a proffered opinion about an opportunity proposed for exploiting, with the goal of supporting the growth aspirations of a business.

Selection of the Preferred Alternative

Commonly, the preferred option is the option which most closely satisfies the project's objectives. It will only be the preferred option if the extent of risk exposure it attracts does not make it less attractive than its nearest rival. Risk exposure can be measured in a number of individual ways or in pre-determined combinations. Risk exposure might be measured in terms of environmental incidents, loss of customers, safety incidents, operational reliability, maintainability or capital expenditure.

Acceptance and Implementation

Having developed a preferred option, the next important step is acceptance finding. The option may have considerable merit; however, it still needs to be acceptable to the project sponsor.

CASE STUDY 22 – NASA RIDM, US

Initial NASA risk management processes were based on continuous risk management (CRM), which stressed the management of risk during implementation. In December 2008, NASA introduced Risk-Informed Decision Making (RIDM)[1] as a complementary process to CRM, which was concerned with the analysis of important and/or direction-setting decisions. Before the introduction of RIDM, risk management was considered equivalent to CRM; now risk management is defined as being composed of both CRM and RIDM. NASA declare that its RIDM process attempts to respond to some of the primary issues that have derailed programmes in the past, namely: (1) the "mismatch" between stakeholder expectations and the "true" resources required to address the risks to achieve those expectations; (2) the lack of comprehension of the risk that a decision maker is accepting when making commitments to stakeholders; and (3) the miscommunication in considering the respective risks associated with competing alternatives. NASA declares that:

> *Risk-Informed Decision Making is distinguished from risk-based decision making in that RIDM is fundamentally a deliberative process that uses a diverse set of performance measures, along with other considerations, to inform decision making. The RIDM process acknowledges the role that human judgment plays in decisions, and that technical information cannot be the sole basis for decision making. This is not only because of inevitable gaps in the technical information, but also because decision making is an inherently subjective, values-based enterprise. In the face of complex decision making involving multiple competing objectives, the cumulative wisdom provided by experienced personnel is essential for integrating technical and nontechnical factors to produce sound decisions.*

---

1   *NASA Risk-Informed Decision Making Handbook*, NASA/SP-2010-576, Version 1.0, April 2010.

The effective evaluation of options requires a comparison of the risk exposure and opportunity that each presents, as simply examining potential revenues and capital expenditure can be dangerously misleading.

☑ Project outcomes are enriched by implementing lessons learned

Sharing lessons learned can reduce risk, improve efficiency, promote validated processes, and improve performance.

NASA, Audit Report March 2012,
review of NASA's lessons learned information system

For those sponsoring projects to learn from the past and understand why some projects fail and others succeed is of paramount importance. As a consequence of the visible trend in the increase in the financial value of projects, project failure can affect shareholders, organisational prosperity and, for major projects, the economy of the region within which the project resides. Lessons learned can be used as an important management tool to support successful project delivery by providing insights into the root causes of both success and failure. While they support the retention of organisational knowledge, they are instrumental in improving project performance by reducing risk exposure. They accomplish this by enhancing risk identification. Any gaps in identification will limit the effectiveness of the overall risk management process. As the old adage goes, unidentified risks are unmanaged risks. The anxiety is that the gaps may include the most serious areas of risk exposure. An analogy can be drawn with the medical profession. A doctor's examination must be thorough prior to making a diagnosis and recommending treatment. Unchecked symptoms may lead to a quick and serious deterioration in a patient's condition. Similarly, poor project risk identification can detrimentally affect a project's health and longevity.

NASA defines lessons learned "as knowledge or understanding gained by experience". This definition is appealing in its simplicity and ease of comprehension. The primary benefit of lessons learned is the combined avoidance of previous problems and the successful repetition of positive achievements. However, the idea of lessons learned is more than just to capture what went well and what should not be repeated. It is a process.

It requires the identification, collection, validation, assessment, classification and sharing of knowledge gleaned through experience. The process of lessons learned is not constrained to one area of a project, but can relate to numerous stages, such as funding, approvals, design, tender action, execution, testing, commissioning and/or handover. As the *PMBOK Guide* recommends, documenting lessons learned should apply throughout the PLC. The process can be conducted prior to the commencement of any stage in the PLC as part of a stage gate review or at project close out.

The usefulness of lessons learned will be determined by their relevance (to future projects), age (the time that has elapsed since their capture), clarity, degree of detail, cross-reference to standards or codes, ease of retrieval (access) and breadth of subjects addressed. It should also contain a description of problems relating to, for instance, the organisational structure, level of resourcing, roles that were overwhelmed, procedures that did not work and required changing, software that did not perform as expected and unanticipated peaks in workload.

Retrieval will be determined by where the lessons have been captured. PRINCE2[17] describes the preparation of a "Lessons Learned Log" which acts as a repository that is populated with lessons learned during a project that can be readily applied to other projects. It advises that as a minimum, the log should be updated at the end of each project stage. A log, record or schedule of lessons should contain not just the more obvious abnormal adverse events, such as abortive design, protracted approvals or contract delays. Appendix I illustrates a possible log for lessons learned.

The saving of lessons learned on a database offers a significant number of benefits, particularly where the population of specific fields is made mandatory. The inclusion of mandatory fields means that the lesson cannot be saved without the capture of pre-determined information. This could include the date of entry, originator, project, project stage, related lessons, related technical specifications or contracts, method of resolution and so on. In summary, it means that the lessons are captured in a consistent manner, can be cross-referenced, can be readily and quickly searched for and can be made accessible to large groups. Documenting a useful lesson learned requires a clear understanding of how it would be applied to a future project.

---

17 Office of Government Commerce (2005) *Managing Successful Projects with PRINCE2*. London: The Stationery Office.

For a lesson learned to be beneficial and of value to others in addressing similar situations, the statements must:

- identify the project management stage during which the problem arose;

- identify the project disciplines affected;

- describe how the problem or opportunity arose (i.e. the catalyst);

- identify the stakeholders involved (for instance, the sponsor, designer, contractor, supplier, local authority or approving body);

- define the problem or positive development encountered; and

- provide concrete, practical solutions or recommendations based on this experience.

However, the application of lessons learned is rarely straightforward. As identified by Gray, "unfortunately when it comes to project management, many organisations don't have the time, discipline or procedures to document lessons learned".[18]

For immature organisations undertaking similar projects where past errors are repeated, the usual root cause is that lessons:

- are learned but not captured;

- are captured but poorly recorded;

- are comprehensively recorded but not placed in context, validated, analysed or cross-referenced; and

- are not readily accessible.

Statements such as "Clearly defined roles and responsibilities leads to effective project management" or "Clearly defined contracts reduce disputes" are not effective lessons learned. There is no context for the statement and,

---

18 Gray, R. (2009) "Implementing a Lessons Learned Knowledge Base", http://www.pmhub.net/wp/2009/05/ron-gray-implementing-a-lessons-learned-knowledge-base.

without context, such a statement serves only as a basic project management best practice. While requiring more effort to develop, the examples in the appendix make the same statement, but do so in a context that defines what project management element is affected by the lesson learned, what the problem was that led to the lesson being learned and how the lesson learned can serve future projects before a problem arises. The success of lessons learned can be hampered if team members:

- are reluctant to search the database as they believe it will not cover the subjects they are interested in and hence will not be fruitful;

- are reluctant to give up their knowledge as they consider it will give them an advantage over colleagues at the time of bonus payments or when competing for management positions;

- are unwilling to share those aspects of their project that did not go well as they will be effectively broadcasting possible mistakes, failures, errors of judgement and/or an inability to manage stakeholders.

An example of a project which has benefited from and has successfully applied lessons learned is the bus rapid transit project carried out in Tanzania by the Rapid Transit Agency and described in Case Study 23. The project proactively sought to learn from seven completed bus projects, focusing on the project in Bogotá, Columbia in particular.

CASE STUDY 23 – BUS RAPID TRANSIT (BRT) PROJECT, DAR ES SALAAM, TANZANIA

The much-needed Dar es Salaam BRT project is currently being implemented by the Dar es Salaam Rapid Transport (DART) agency in Dar es Salaam (the largest city of Tanzania). The project is aligned to Tanzania's development strategy, which underscores the need for improved transport infrastructure to achieve specific social and economic objectives. The overall DART system is being developed in six phases involving six main corridors and arterial roads in Dar es Salaam. The completed network will be composed of 137 kilometres of bus corridors, 228 stations, 18 terminals and a number of depots. The BRT system will be operated by a public-private partnership (PPP) arrangement with two private bus operators, one fare collector and a fund manager. Prior to the commencement of the design (as reported by Cosmas Takule, the Chief

Executive of the Dar Rapid Transit Agency), the Agency sought technical support from UITP[1] and UATP,[2] and examined the lessons learned from existing bus systems in Columbia, Peru, Venezuela, Chile, Mexico, Guatemala and Ecuador. The BRT project was designed by Logit of Brazil in association with Interconsult of Tanzania,[3] which adopted lessons from the TransMilenio, a BRT system that serves Bogotá, the capital of Colombia. Bogotá had provided proof that the BRT concept is capable of delivering high-capacity performance for the world's mega-cities. In addition, conceptual planning of the Tanzania BRT was assisted by TransMilenio officials Enrique Peñalosa, the Mayor of Bogotá from 1998 to 2001 who implemented TransMilenio, and Edgar Sandoval, TransMilenio's first manager.[4] The World Bank Country Director for Tanzania, Mr John McIntire, said that Tanzania had emulated other mega-cities in the world that have introduced the similar systems.[5] However, while experience was sought from other cities, there was a recognition that it needed to be tailored to the project. In particular, early planning sought to ensure that engineering did not take place in isolation from its context and took cognisance of the financial, environmental and legal constraints. Moreover, there was an appreciation that a special purpose agency and decision-making structures should be established early and priority should be given to regulatory issues. Special purpose teams for system planning and implementation were created. The overall aim of these actions was to reduce the risk of schedule overrun and/or cost increases, and to provide reassurance to the funders, the most significant of which is the World Bank.

---

1   UITP is the international organisation for public transport authorities and operators.
2   UATP is the African Association of Public Transport.
3   Wa Simbeye, Finnigan (2013) "WB Defends Redesigning Dar Bus Rapid Project", *Daily News*, 19 January.
4   "BRT in Dar es Salaam", http://ansoncfit.com/watson/brt-in-dar-es-salaam.
5   Rugonzibwa, Pius (2010) "Rapid Transit System Project Takes Off", *Daily News*, 10 August.

For new projects, a review of the lessons learned from previous similar projects can significantly enhance the risk identification process.

☑ Risk analysis needs to recognise the existence of optimism bias

> Bias entails a value-directed departure from accuracy, objectivity, and balance – not just a distorted presentation of facts.
>
> Stephen Klaidman,
> former editor of the New York Times and the Washington Post

Optimism bias, for those not familiar with the term, may be described as the demonstrated systematic tendency for appraisers to be overly optimistic about key project implementation parameters, including capital costs, operating costs, works duration and benefits delivery.

Government departments and organisations sponsoring projects seek to ensure that funds are expended in the most efficient way. This efficiency drive requires an analytically robust appraisal of proposals before significant funds are committed. Appraisal typically entails examining the initial CAPEX (capital expenditure), future cashflow (revenue), OPEX (operating expenditure) and maintenance costs. However, systemic optimism ("optimism bias") has historically plagued the appraisal process, whereby outturn CAPEX and project delivery durations have both repeatedly and significantly exceeded initial appraisal estimates.

Optimism bias is described by the UK government's HM Treasury as the tendency for a project's costs and duration to be underestimated and/or the project benefits to be overestimated. Optimism specific to cost is expressed as the percentage difference between the estimate at the appraisal stage and the final outturn cost. Likewise, optimism specific to time is expressed as the percentage difference between the schedule duration at the appraisal stage and the final outturn duration. Studies have shown that optimism bias is caused by a failure to identify and effectively manage project risk. HM Treasury's *The Green Book, Appraisal and Evaluation in Central Government* records that "there is a demonstrated, systematic, tendency for project appraisers to be overly optimistic". The new edition of *The Green Book*, published in 2003, includes for the first time an explicit adjustment procedure to redress what it describes as the systematic optimism ("optimism bias") or misplaced confidence that over recent years has bedevilled the appraisal process. It advises that to reduce this tendency, "appraisers should make explicit adjustments in the form of increasing estimates of the costs and decreasing and delaying the receipt of estimated benefits". In addition, the department recommends that adjustments for optimism bias should be empirically based on adopting data from past projects or similar projects elsewhere which is adjusted for the unique characteristics of the project in hand. A recent example of the application of optimism bias is described in Case Study 24, whereby a significant adjustment was made to the predicted outturn infrastructure costs by the addition of costs arising from optimism bias and risk exposure.

CASE STUDY 24 – PROPOSED HS2 RAILWAY, ENGLAND

Within the report prepared by HS2 Ltd[1] commissioned by the Department for Transport for the controversial new HS2 railway line, it described its approach to calculating risk exposure. The report states the costs for Phase 1, London–West Midlands (currently developed to a higher level of detail than the cost of the rest of the Y network), include what it terms as "a full Quantitative Risk Assessment (QRA)", which incorporates an assessment of optimism bias. The report records that the total allowance for risk and optimism bias for Phase 1 is equivalent to an additional 64 per cent of the infrastructure costs. The report adds that (at the time of writing) a quantitative risk analysis had not been undertaken for routes to Manchester and Leeds, hence the full 66 per cent optimism bias that has been applied to Phase 2 costs in line with HM Treasury guidance.

---

1   HS2 Ltd (2012) *Economic Case for HS2: Updated Appraisal of Transport User Benefits and Wider Economic Benefits*, report to the government by HS2 Ltd, January 2012. This report was commissioned by the Department for Transport (DfT).

Monitoring

It is assumed that once the sponsor has committed funds to the project, the sponsor will monitor its delivery using (as a minimum) the optimism bias *Risk Area Contributors* to guide data gathering and risk management practices, and, in addition, that this monitoring will run through each stage gate review and the sponsor will expect to see evidence that the most likely cost estimate (or PMean) has been adjusted downwards to reflect the developing experience and improved knowledge of the project.

Using Numerical Indicators in Project Decision Making

The adoption of a methodology to address optimism bias is intended to develop a robust approach to the assessment of the capital cost of public projects in order to determine whether the project should be supported. The approach is based on the project team preparing the business case reflecting on the following questions and understanding to what extent they have been answered:

- Are the stakeholders and their requirements known?

- Is the scope clearly defined?

- Are the boundaries of the project clearly defined?

- What project information is not available and as a result what assumptions were made?

- What is the potential range of possible outcomes for each of the assumptions?

- Is the risk exposure profile of the project fully understood?

- Are the major risks identified manageable?

- How will the risk exposure profile change over time?

- Has the source of the funding been made explicit?

- Will the source of funding be annualised?

- Will the project involve novel technology?

Proposed changes to the project during its life cycle should be assessed against the original business case to establish if the scheme is more or less attractive and whether the business case is undermined or not as a result.

Causes of Optimism Bias

Comprehension of the causes of optimism bias is important to ensure that the drivers are responded to and to reduce the potential exposure to surprises in terms of the outturn cost and duration.

From its analysis, Mott MacDonald[19] found that the top 11 *Risk Area Contributors* which led to an increase in capital expenditure arising from optimism bias are those listed below (in descending order of frequency of occurrence). All of the *risk areas* were addressed in Case Study 25 with the greatest risk exposure emanating from "Economic" factors, such as a change in raw material costs, fluctuations in the currency exchange rate and an increase in tender prices unrelated to inflation:

1. Inadequacy of the business case (58 per cent).

2. Environmental impact (19 per cent).

3. Disputes and claims (16 per cent).

4. Economic (13 per cent).

5. Late contractor involvement in design (12 per cent).

6. Complexity of contract structure (11 per cent).

7. Legislation (7 per cent).

8. Degree of innovation (7 per cent).

9. Poor contractor capabilities (6 per cent).

10. Project management team (4 per cent).

11. Poor project intelligence (4 per cent).

---

19 MacDonald, M. (2002) *Review of Large Public Procurement in the UK*, July, undertaken on behalf of HM Treasury, UK.

BUSINESS CASE

With reference to item 1 above, the Mott MacDonald study states that "in most instances, the inadequacy of the business case was stated to be the major cause of project time and cost overruns" (section 2.4.3, p. 17). It goes on to state that: "This fundamentally demonstrates the need to concentrate significant effort and diligence to ensure the business case comprehensively represents the requirements of all of the project stakeholders in terms of the agreed scope and objectives." It also says that "most of the traditionally procured projects in the sample were inadequately defined (in terms of requirements and project scope) in the approved business case".

The Distinction between Risk Events and Optimism Bias

The critical issue to avoid in a project appraisal is being overly pessimistic by double-counting risk exposure through the addition of quantitative risk analysis results with optimism bias figures, which are based on the same risks. The UK Department for Transport (DfT) guide recommends the addition of the PMean quantitative risk analysis output with the mitigated optimism bias figure. One possible method is to restrict the risk assessment to purely technical risks and the optimism bias figure to business case issues (such as income and operational, maintenance and renewal costs). It is assumed that the project promoter will confirm acceptance (or otherwise) of the split of risk categories in terms of those incorporated within the quantitative risk analysis and those included in the optimism bias assessment. The example described in Case Study 25 consciously ensured that there was no double-counting of the risk exposure (i.e. overlapping of optimism bias and the QRA).

CASE STUDY 25 – ABU DHABI METRO, UNITED ARAB EMIRATES

A business case was prepared on behalf of the Abu Dhabi Department of Transport (DoT) for a metro network that would provide a high-capacity, high-quality rapid transit service linking major activity centers in the metropolitan region. To support the development of the business case, a risk assessment was undertaken of project delivery risk, optimism bias and the cost of risk response planning. The approach followed was to adopt the UK DfT's method of estimating outturn capital expenditure as a comparator to the US Federal Transit Administration's New Start approach to business case appraisal. The DfT approach is based on the UK HM Treasury's guidance on project appraisal

---

described in *The Green Book*[1] and supplementary papers.[2] This guidance recommends that projects make explicit adjustments to the estimate of costs for risk exposure based on the aggregated assessment of delivery risk exposure as measured by quantitative risk analysis, mitigated optimism bias and the cost of response planning. The assessment of risk followed this guidance.[3] The guidance reinforced the view that a risk assessment was a key component of the business case analysis to provide an analytically robust approach to both the appraisal and the feasibility assessment process. It was considered that a risk assessment would support a more vigorous analysis of CAPEX by identifying the commonly occurring risks that expose projects to a reduction in quality, an increase in expenditure and a delay in handover. A risk assessment is only meaningful and valid if it is aligned to a project's scope, budget, timeframe and anticipated procurement route. Each of these aspects of the project was described within the business case. The business case recorded that upon the approval to proceed, the most fundamental decision that would need to be taken on the project would be the method of project procurement and delivery. The risk assessment assumed that the works would be delivered by a single design-and-build engineer-procure-construct (EPC) contract based on conditions laid down by the Internal Federation of Consulting Engineers (FIDIC). It was noted that these conditions could obviously be modified by the DoT to suit its desire to transfer the majority of the execution risk to the contractor. The business case recorded that the DoT and Abu Dhabi government maintained a risk-averse position. The risk assessment also assumed that the preliminary design would be undertaken by the DoT's consultant, whereafter the consultant's drawings and specifications would form part of the tender documentation. These were important foundation stones for the risk assessment in terms of which party would carry particular risks. Risk identification was carried out with the aid of a risk breakdown structure (RBS) to strive to ensure that the risk identification process was comprehensive and did not leave any "blind spots" (overlooked areas of exposure). The compilation of the risk register was based on a number of underlying assumptions and these were stated in the assessment. The quantitative cost risk analysis (QCRA) was performed using the Palisade software tool @RISK for Excel (version 5.5.0, 2009) in accordance with the project's Risk Management Plan. The modelling assumptions were provided together with an explanation of the operation of the Monte Carlo simulation technique which supported the preparation of the QCRA. The risk-adjusted results produced by the Federal Transit Administration and the UK DfT approaches were very similar.

---

1   HM Treasury (2003) *The Green Book*. London: The Stationery Office.

2   HM Treasury (2003) *Supplementary Green Book Guidance on Optimism Bias*, https://www.gov.uk/government/publications/green-book-supplementary-guidance-optimism-bias.

3   The DfT guidance recommends the adoption of the PMean as opposed to, for example, the 70th or 75th percentile of the results. PMean is the term used to describe the arithmetic mean of the results of a quantitative risk simulation. The risk assessment drew attention to the fact that in adopting the PMean, there was a 50 per cent chance that this figure could be exceeded and hence it was not a conservative figure.

> Adjusting project costs and benefits for optimism bias provides sponsors of capital projects with greater certainty in terms of outturn costs and the preservation of business case objectives.

☑ The workshop "circus" is avoided by recognising behaviour types

> *Workshops have the potential to liberate new ideas which can bring about remarkable change.*
>
> Robert Chapman, author

You thought you would be running a workshop, but in the end found you were trying to herd a colony of feral cats. One of the pre-requisites of running a workshop is to anticipate common behaviour types. A number of psychologists have described behavioural differences between team members. Dr David Merill, an industrial psychologist, developed a simple approach and describes people as falling into four approximate profiles or zones[20] (numerous others have subsequently produced a variation on the original ideas). The four zones when assembled in a square form a universe of human personality with a distinct north, east, south and west, to which managers can readily relate (see Figure 8.10 below). From right to left, it measures assertiveness, from passivity to activity, or from "asking" to "telling". From the top to bottom, it measures responsiveness, i.e. whether we react in a controlled fashion (top) or in an emotional fashion (bottom). Thus, an "Analytical" is a combination of reactive and task-oriented. A "Driver" is a combination of task-oriented and proactive. An "Amiable" profile is people-orieated and reactive, while an "Expressive" is a combination of proactive and people-oriented. As you might imagine, people are far too complicated to fit neatly into a single box. However, most of us have a dominant personality type, with one or two secondary types, all of which can change and evolve over time. It's generally not too difficult to identify the primary personality type of an individual, based on his or her temperament, behaviour, communication style and to some extent profession. The mix of personality types in a workshop will have a direct impact on its outcome.

---

20 Merill, D.W. and Reid, R.H. (1999) *Personal Styles and Effective Performance*. London: CRC Press.

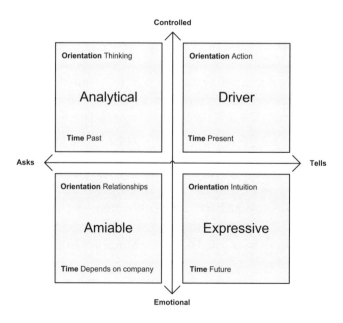

Figure 8.10   Four personality profiles

Analyticals dislike making decisions prematurely. They are less tuned into theoretical concepts and extrapolations than other profile types. They like to consider the facts before taking action. They place a premium on accuracy and expect it from others. Hence, they like a lot of background details in order to make decisions – information is their comfort zone. For this reason, decisions can take a long time, because they need to be sure. They are not strong at thinking about future potential problems or making subjective assessments that require approximations, especially if answers are needed quickly. Their key virtue is patience, but their caution can appear to other profile types as paralysis. They like detailed reports and well-reasoned conclusions and recommendations. They will talk through points at length, often frustrating the Driver and Expressive personality types. They are often happiest working alone. Don't ask them to make a subjective assessment about the financial impact of a risk in a workshop. You are likely to get a quick, abrupt and unhelpful reply, like "I do not do guess work".

Drivers are project director personality types. They are uncomfortable sitting on the sidelines and are prone to want to "steal the show". They have a propensity to want to dominate a discussion and drive home their viewpoint. They are firmly rooted in the present moment and have a penchant for direct action. They are natural leaders, making decisions quickly and delegating naturally. They are fast-moving and results-driven, and are frequently frustrated by the preference of Analyticals for caution and detail. They are good at both setting and adhering to objectives and deadlines. They are generally good motivators of project teams. They can be prone to aggression and to leaving people behind as they forge ahead and drive through obstacles. However, they will deliver the project safely, on time, under budget and to the required quality standards. All objectives are generally exceeded, but there may be a few notable casualties along the way. As they say, they bring home the bacon. However, they have a short attention span, do not want to be distracted by inordinate detail and are results-oriented. Hence, they are more receptive to discussing the most serious risks on a project and the proposed response actions rather than building the risk register from the basement up.

Amiable personality types are essentiality "people focused" and are considerate of other team members. Highly responsive, they are sensitive to others' feelings and are notably patient. They are planners as well as well as "doers" and are cheerful completers. Their great strength is their understanding of relationships. They are familiar with not only the organisational structure but also the external stakeholders. They are good coordinators precisely because they take time to understand who is doing what and touch base with all affected disciplines and stakeholders. They make the best stakeholder managers. They are the backbone of any project, making sure everyone who needs to be informed or consulted about something is informed or consulted. They are tolerant and will be the quickest to forgive the excesses of the other styles. Hence, they will not sink into a stony silence in workshops if they think they have been belittled by the Drivers. They will work until the job is done. They appreciate being asked for their opinion or for help, and can take a lot of responsibility. Without them, no work would get completed. However, they dislike uncertainty and prefer clear direction. As such, if you include them in a workshop, make sure the objectives are clear, that there is a defined structure and that the task you are trying to complete in the timeframe is realistic.

Expressive personality types are essentially big picture and future-oriented. Of all the profiles, they are generally the ones with the most cheerful disposition. They are sociable, convivial and likely to be the loudest voices in the office. Along with Amiables, they are those with the best networks. They are the ones most likely to drag everyone off to a restaurant or a party at the end of a hard day. They will be impatient and will finish your sentence. They are imaginative and creative, taking the ideas of others and developing them into something previously unconsidered. They are approximate, fast-moving, broad-brush and forward-thinking. They don't do detail and they loathe having to slow down. They tend not to deal with conflict well because they want everyone to be in agreement and work in a relaxed atmosphere. Ultimately, they live for recognition, preferably if it is shown publicly. A workshop attended by just Expressives would be pleasant and frustrating all at the same time. They will see risk management as a dry subject. They will want to dominate the conversation at workshops and will be restless with a desire to complete quickly. A workshop attended by just Expressive and Driver personality types would force the risk process to be split. They would not want to get bogged down in detail. The assessment of probabilities and impacts, the assignment of actionees, defining detailed response actions or planned completion dates would have to be undertaken with a different group.

Commonly, project teams have all of these behavioural types mixed together and we expect them to work together in risk workshops, interviews and meetings. Robbins and Finley provide some helpful guidance in terms of working with the different personality types which have been tailored here to the workshop setting:

With Analyticals, strive to do the following:

- make sure you have prepared for the workshop;

- describe your objectives and the desired output of the workshop;

- share your programme of activities;

- avoid disorganisation or mistakes in terms of detail or presentation as they will quickly lose interest;

- work through the workshop in a methodical manner;

- share the output of lessons learned;

- be equipped with a risk breakdown structure, checklists and outputs of previous projects;

- cover all of the primary sources of risk;

- assign actionees who will prepare response actions to the risks identified;

- be clear and precise in everything you do;

- bring the discussion back if it has strayed on to an irrelevant subject;

- avoid discussions which have no factual basis.

With Drivers, strive to do the following:

- be short, sharp and succinct when setting the scene;

- be clear about the end gain, the objectives you want to achieve and why;

- avoid long introductions at all costs;

- if you ask project discipline leaders to set the scene at the outset, make sure they keep to their allotted time – be ruthless;

- rehearse the benefits of risk management and how they will be accomplished;

- make sure you understand the context of the project – do your homework. Do not ask basic questions about the project that you should have gleaned already;

- do not try to be too "bossy" as Drivers do not like to be driven;

- if you disagree with a comment, base your response on hard facts;

- quickly move attendees along if the discussion has turned into a detailed discussion about a topic or risk;

- remind attendees of the time elapsed, the time remaining and the tasks still to be accomplished.

With Amiables, strive to do the following:

- be informal;

- describe the approach being adopted and the required end results;

- ask "why" questions to draw out their opinions;

- define how you want them to participate and contribute;

- explain that the risk process is aimed at reaching a consensus on the risk exposure and that the sources of risks do not need to be recorded;

- quickly defuse any arguments and press the antagonists to take their subject "offline" for a separate discussion after the workshop;

- listen and be responsive;

- avoid a highly structured regimental command of the workshop as Amiables will "tune out".

With Expressives, strive to do the following:

- meet their social needs, entertain, stimulate and be lively where possible;

- take time – they are most efficient when not in a hurry;

- ask for their opinion and ideas;

- keep your eye on the big picture and not the details – what are likely to be the major problems/risks that may be encountered?;

- consider having multiple workshops. Leave discussion on the risk impacts and response actions for separate workshops with the Analyticals and follow up with a consensus meeting at a later date;

- share examples from other projects naming individuals they might know and respect;

- show honest respect – Expressives do not like being talked down to.

The key is to learn how to connect to each of the profiles and how best to get them to cooperate and participate in the risk management process not just once but on an ongoing basis.

> Anticipate and reflect in your approach the existence of very different behaviour types.

☑ Project success and particularly risk management is dependent on proactive behaviour

> *Project managers want to act, not be acted upon. Being a proactive manager means taking control of a project rather than letting events, conditions or others take control.*
>
> Robert Chapman, author

When considering the projects of today, how much time is spent looking ahead and how much time is spent reacting to events? At the very core of effective risk management is the need for a proactive culture – a culture where project team members consciously apply their knowledge and experience (lessons learned) by proactively striving to avoid past problems and repeat former successes. Being proactive is described in the *Oxford Pocket Dictionary of Current English* (2009) as "creating or controlling a situation by causing something to happen rather than responding to it after it has happened". Academics expand on this simple statement by describing the act of being proactive as making things happen, anticipating and preventing problems, and seizing opportunities. They believe it involves self-initiated efforts to bring about change in the work environment and/or oneself to achieve a different future. The prolific authors Parker, Bindl and Strauss identify proactivity as a goal-driven process involving both the setting of a proactive goal (proactive goal generation) and striving to achieve that proactive goal (proactive goal striving).[21] Proactive goal generation has been described as involving at least two processes: envisioning and planning.[22] Envisioning involves perceiving a current or future problem or opportunity and imagining a different future that can be achieved by actively addressing this problem or opportunity.[23] Having envisaged a different future, the process of planning involves the individual deciding on which actions to take to achieve this future. Proactive goal striving is defined as the behavioural and psychological mechanisms by which individuals purposively seek to accomplish productive goals. It is interesting to note that organisational research on the subject of the proactive behaviour of individuals within organisations has truly blossomed, the reason being that proactive behaviour is seen as an increasingly important component of job performance with the potential to be a "high leverage" concept. The organisational literature portrays proactive behaviours as prevalent at work and as affecting outcomes for both the individuals who carry them out and their organisations. Within his book *The Seven Habits of Highly Effective People*, Steven Covey[24] describes Habit 1 as "Be Proactive". He contrasts being proactive or having a proactive mentality with being reactive. Reactive people, he says, are those who are resigned to the notion that whatever they do, they can have no effect on their circumstances. Proactive people, on the other hand, having a particular attitude of mind can make a huge and positive difference.

When teams of people are proactive and forward-looking, they are far more successful at delivering projects than those which are not. The example of the Holyrood Project given in Case Study 10 (and continued below) is an example of a project where the absence of formal proactive action can have a detrimental influence on project performance.

The former Office of Government Commerce (OGC) identified within its procurement guide[25] proactive integrated supply teams (ISTs) as efficient delivery agents for projects. In the context of construction projects, the OGC

21 Parker, K.S., Bindl, U.K and Strauss, K. (2010) "Making Things Happen: A Model of Proactive Motivation", *Journal of Management*, 36(4), 827–56.

22 Bindl, U.K. and Parker, K.S. (2009) "Phases of Proactivity: How Do We Actually Go the Extra Mile?", paper presented to the European Congress of Work and Organisational Psychology, Spain.

23 French, R. et al. (2011) *Organizational Behaviour*, 2nd edn. Chichester: John Wiley & Sons.

24 *The Seven Habits of Highly Effective People* has sold more than 25 million copies in 38 languages worldwide. In August 2011, Time listed it as one of "The 25 Most Influential Business Management Books". It is reported that US President Bill Clinton read the book and invited Covey to Camp David to counsel him on how to integrate the book into his presidency.

25 OGC (2003) *Achieving Excellence in Construction Procurement Guide 05: The Integrated Project Team: Teamworking and Partnering*.

considers that there may be a number of specialised supply chains delivering design services, construction services and product suppliers (providing components manufactured and assembled off-site). Each supply chain member should be accustomed to working together as part of a fully linked chain. The individual supply chains must be integrated together so that collectively they represent all the parties responsible for delivering a specific product or service.

The guide states that three key criteria for selecting the IST are:

- a proven attitude to collaborative working and integrated approach;

- a proven ability to be proactive; and

- a proven track record in innovation and managing risk.

The parallels between proactive behaviour and risk management are clear to see, for the very essence of risk management requires (when considering threats or downside risks) looking ahead to recognise potential adverse events and responding to them before they bite. How project team members think ahead, perceive and respond to potential threats is as important as the risks themselves. Even when risks are identified, a lack of inertia can lead to a lack of treatment. This can be just as debilitating for projects as risks that remain unidentified. Accenture[26] believes proactive behaviour is exhibited by the "procurement masters". This is the term they apply to those organisations which are high performers in procurement risk management due to their implementation of the risk management stages of "anticipating", "monitoring" and "mitigation".[27]

In terms of upside risks, this means recognising potential opportunities to investigate and exploit for the benefit of a project's objectives. Hence, risk management is not about detached inactive or passive observation, but informed proactive intervention. It involves aspiring and striving to bring about change in the project environment to achieve a different future. Proactive individuals are recognised as having three key attributes:

---

26 Accenture is a global management consultancy, technical services and outsourcing company.

27 Accenture (2010) "High Performance in Procurement Risk Management: Research and Insights Developed in Collaboration with Massachusetts Institute of Technology", http://www.accenture.com/SiteCollectionDocuments/PDF/Accenture_High_Performance_in_Procurement_Risk_Management.pdf.

self-starting, change-oriented and future-focused. Being proactive is not just confined to individuals. For organisations, proactive project teams (with shared goals) are recognised as having three similar attributes. They have a propensity to be future-focused (engaging in forethought), to possess insight (derived from knowledge and experience) and to be change-oriented (seeking to avoid disruptive events).

There are important lessons that can be drawn from the recent financial crisis that are translatable to projects teams. There are clear examples of proactive and passive teams within the investment banks. After the financial crisis of 2008, as you would imagine, there has been a high degree of introspection among investors, investment banks, regulators, central banks and governments. Researchers have found that good leadership clearly made a difference, especially in terms of the adoption of robust risk management. Many of the businesses and public sector organisations which emerged unscathed from the financial tsunami had seen the dangers looming on the horizon. It has come to light that their staff not only understood the risks to their own organisation but also recognised the wider implications of these events and took immediate steps to circumnavigate them. Essentially, these organisations had cultures not only attuned to the potential risks but also to being proactive in addressing them. By contrast, those who suffered the most during the crisis did not appear to anticipate the risks ahead, especially the risks that would spread with alarming speed across both markets and borders. Sir John Gieve (the then Deputy Governor of the Bank of England) stated that the weakness in the English banking system "was the failure of banks and many other investors to appreciate, price and manage risk". He explained that the bank's systems were preparing them for a shower, not a hurricane.

When people speak about the investment banks and companies which fared so poorly during the crisis, the most important questions revolve around risk. How could they not have known the risks? If they had known, why didn't they react sooner? Was the reliance they placed on their sophisticated statistical techniques for measuring risk exposure flawed? Was it safe to base predictions about the future on observations of the past? What were their own economists saying and were they being heeded or ignored? Were they riding a wave of unprecedented growth that they thought would never end? Why didn't they understand the ramifications of their actions? Could they not foresee how their decisions would inevitably ripple across companies and countries to affect others? The declaration made by the G20[28] at its summit held in Washington DC on 15 November 2008 stated that market participants (including investment banks) had an inadequate appreciation of the risks, failed to exercise due diligence, had unsound risk management practices and did not adequately appreciate and address the risks. Clearly, the investment teams of banks had failed to manage effectively.

Table 8.3 includes the primary causes of bank failure during the credit crisis of 2008 where proactive behaviour and formal risk management had been inadequate and the implications for PRM.

28 The G20 is made up of the finance ministries and central bank governors of 20 economies: Argentina, Australia, Brazil, Canada, China, France, Germany, India, Indonesia, Italy, Japan, the Republic of Korea, Mexico, Russia, Saudi Arabia, South Africa, Turkey, the UK, the US and the European Union. It is a forum for cooperation and consultation on matters relating to the international financial system. It studies, reviews and promotes a high-level discussion on policy issues relating to the promotion of international financial stability and as a consequence seeks to address issues that go beyond the responsibilities of any one organisation.

Table 8.3   Causes of bank failure during the credit crisis and the lessons for PRM

Lessons from the financial crisis	Background to the lessons drawn from the financial crisis	What it means for PRM
Short observation periods	Bank risk analysts used the results of movement in the markets from very short observation periods to make predictions about the future.	Proactive behaviour would look at the success or otherwise of similar projects organisation-wide (and, where appropriate, nationally and internationally) together with government publications (if advantageous to do so) to glean lessons learned.
Non-normal distributions	Banks underestimated the impact of very low-probability but very high-impact risks.	The incorporation of these events into simulations (quantitative analysis) without well-considered modelling (i.e. choice of probabilities and distributions) could lead to recommendations regarding contingencies which were too low. Proactive behaviour would involve constructing the models in a number of ways to arrive at reliable, defensible results.
Systemic as opposed to idiosyncratic risk	There are nine recognised drivers of systemic risk. Interconnectedness is one of the recognised drivers and is generally measured by consideration of counterparty risks related to a financial institution's activities. Knowledge of the interconnectedness of a financial institution would have assisted in determining how many additional failures could be caused by the failure of an individual firm.	A risk for projects is default by a designer, contractor, major subcontractor or supplier. Proactive behaviour would include the vetting of contractors, for instance, during the prequalification process to establish their financial stability, any current litigation in which they are embroiled and the current position of their order books. Another risk for projects is similar concurrent projects locally, nationally and internationally (as appropriate), which would deplete available resources such as contractors, specialist technology, plant, labour and materials (availability and price). Proactive behaviour would look at the interdependence or interconnectedness between the project under consideration and others with specific regard to, for example, specialist subcontractors, suppliers and material availability.
Drawing inferences about the future from past events	The reliance on past events as a measure of likely future events left banks exposed to errors of judgement.	The economic climate, inflation, emerging novel technology, global and micro-climatic conditions and material availability are constantly changing. Proactive behaviour would lead to an examination of the project context and avoidance of sole reliance on checklists and prompt lists (e.g. SLEPT, PEST, PESTLE, SPECTRUM, TECOP and STEEPLE) based on past experience.

Table 8.3 Causes of bank failure during the credit crisis and the lessons for PRM *concluded*

Lessons from the financial crisis	Background to the lessons drawn from the financial crisis	What it means for PRM
Lack of management comprehension	The statistical models of risk exposure became so sophisticated that they became difficult for risk analysts to explain and for board members to comprehend.	Early use of simulation techniques using proprietary software led sponsors of projects to distrust "black box" outputs as they did not understand how the models were constructed or how the software derived results from the risk spreadsheets. Proactive behaviour would ensure that construction of the risk models and the operation of the software was explained so that decisions could be made on the findings with confidence.
Risk-averse/risk-seeking balance	Banks were so heavily leveraged that as soon as the defaults commenced, they quickly ran into trouble.	Developers at times work on tight margins and the inclusion of what they might consider to be significant or large contingencies within the cost plan would invalidate their business case. Proactive behaviour would ensure that contingencies are created which could absorb unexpected delays or additional costs. The calculation of contingencies should be based on tried-and-tested methods, not heuristics.
Group think	Banks followed the "success" of their competitors (particularly the growth in profits) and, being eager for a slice of the pie, jumped on the bandwagon without understanding where it was headed.	Within projects and particularly construction projects, different forms of contract follow waves of popularity and on occasion the "herd instinct" overrides objective assessment. Consider the popularity of management contracts and partnerships. Proactive behaviour would lead to a risk-based evaluation of alternative procurement routes and forms of contract so that the risk ownership profile is fully understood, particularly in the event that significant adverse events materialise.
Dominant personalities and "club" mentality. No independent challenge	There was a lack of independent constructive challenge to dominant personalities.	Like banks, projects can have their own dominant personalities. Proactive behaviour would lead to seeking out a second (and third) opinion about whether the risks identified within the project business case are comprehensive, have been analysed realistically and evaluated (aggregated together) in a manner which closely resembles how the project would evolve.

CASE STUDY 10 (CONTINUED) – THE HOLYROOD PROJECT, SCOTLAND

As identified and reported by the Auditor General for Scotland in his 2004 report, risk management did not follow, in his words, "good practice". Specifically, the report identified that while 12 risk workshops were held between October and December 2002, leading to the identification and assignment of responsibility for risk responses, there was no monitoring of the effectiveness of the responses. It was not possible to readily discern that the project was implementing proactive risk management to address potential threats to the project objectives. From December 2002, the approach to risk management further deteriorated. The Auditor General stated:

> There were no further workshops with the previous wide participation. There was thereafter no systematic basis for any action by project management to manage out risk, although the cost consultant continued to report its assessment of the cost of risk in accordance with its terms of engagement. In its reports the cost consultant assigned a cost to each risk and reported the total cost, which it called a reserve for outstanding construction items. This reserve was reported in parallel with the cost consultant's report on the current construction commitment and project management generally accepted the combined results of the two reports as the best estimate of the total eventual construction cost. Over time, as individual risks have materialised, the cost consultant has reported a reduction in the total risk reserve offset by a corresponding increase in the cost of the current construction commitment. However for most of the time the cost consultant has also identified and costed new risks, which increased the risk reserve – it was 'topped up', as it were. The net result was that between 2000 and early 2004 there was a steady increase in the overall forecast construction cost. The approach used at Holyrood appears to be an unusual way to manage risks. It seems the approach has been to tacitly accept increases to the cost of the project rather than forcing action to prevent the increases.[1]

1   Audit Scotland (2004) "Management of the Holyrood Building Project", prepared by the Auditor General for Scotland.

Proactive behaviour is the kernel of PRM.

☑ Risk descriptions are improved by adopting a metalanguage

Unambiguous risk descriptions are clearly essential if we are to manage risks effectively.

David Hillson, *leading risk practitioner and author*

The overall effectiveness of risk management and the rate at which it starts to contribute to project management will depend in part at least on the clarity, relevance and objectivity of the information contained in the risk register or risk database. Unfortunately, risk descriptions are often a confused mixture of causes, risks, impacts and background project information. As a consequence, risk registers frequently include items that are not risks, or what the PMI Practice Standard for Project Risk Management describes as "non-risks". How often have you attended a risk workshop and attendees have volunteered threats to the project objectives, such as "schedule overrun", "project budget exceeded" or "quality requirements not met"? How would you characterise these statements? They are clearly impacts or the effect of risks, not risks in themselves. It would not be possible to define a response action (or actions) to a risk called "schedule overrun" without knowing what the event or events were that would result in this impact.

In addition, risk descriptions frequently contain the risk cause. These are the trigger for a risk. Hence, risk descriptions arising from a workshop for a particular construction project such as "national shortage of skilled operatives", "piling subcontractors' poor maintenance of piling rigs" and "poor performance of existing bearing suppliers" are prevailing adverse conditions or events that have already been witnessed or experienced. They are certain, not uncertain. They relate to existing circumstances and not potential events. They are not risks in themselves. However, they will most likely trigger new risk events which threaten the project's objectives.

Risk registers which are a confused mixture of causes, risks and impacts can set back the implementation of risk management. This lack of clarity can lead to:

- an inability to quickly understand the risk event (or events) being proposed;

- a need to question, debate and amend the risk entries;

- a reticence of project team members to invest time in risk management;

- a delay in the definition and implementation of response actions;

- disillusionment among recipients of risk registers as to the value of risk management;

- erosion of the time available to act before critical risks materialise.

Prior to the commencement of risk meetings and workshops with project participants, it is important to articulate the distinction between a cause, risk and impact.

Cause

A cause is a specific event that has materialised or is an existing prevailing condition within the project environment (context) which gives rise to uncertainty. It is certain as it currently exists.

Risk

A risk is an uncertain event that, should it materialise, would affect the project objectives. The risks identified must relate to the project objectives. Hence, a pre-requisite of PRM is to make the project objectives explicit from the outset and ensure they are disseminated to the project team. It would be inappropriate and unproductive for participating team members to spend time identifying risks which are inconsequential to the project's business case, objectives or the prevailing legislation to which it must accord. In addition, risk descriptions must be clear. They must not be so short that they are ambiguous. They must be readily comprehendible to the recipients of the risk register or viewers of the database. When they are short, even the authors of the risks cannot recall a month later what they meant by the risk description. In the context of this rule, risks must not be a confused mixture or causes, risks and impacts.

Impact

An impact is an unplanned variation from the project objectives (either positive or negative) which arises as a result of the risk materialising. Examples include the overall completion date not being achieved, the authorised budget being exceeded, the required quality standards not being realised and breaches of environmental legislation. While project participants can readily identify single risks and their effect, what they are not so capable of understanding is how risks will interact. In other words, how newly identified risks will impact on previously identified risks.

Metalanguage

The use of a metalanguage in the field of risk management is not new. Metalanguage is the use of definitions or opinions about the usage or meaning of words. Linguistics sometimes describes itself as a metalanguage because it is a "language" about language. There are a variety of recognised metalanguages, including *embedded*, *ordered* and *nested* (or *hierarchical*). The metalanguage adopted here is a "risk language" considered to be embedded within the "object language" in order to help project participants readily understand the difference between a cause, risk and impact, and the sequence in which they occur.

Figure 8.11 describes the difference between "cause", "risk" and "impact" for a threat (as opposed to an opportunity). Hence, risk in this instance is labelled as a "pernicious" event, as opposed to an opportunity that a project would seek to exploit.

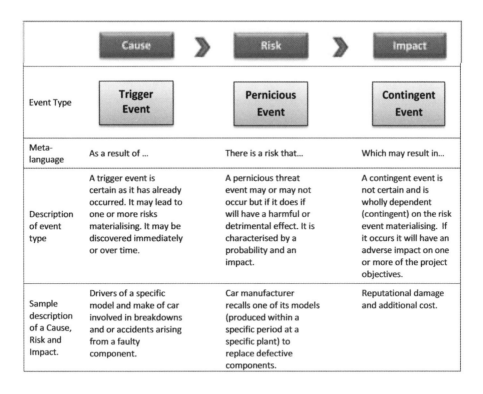

Figure 8.11   Distinguishing between cause, risk and impact

Poor risk descriptions can undermine the adoption and hence the effectiveness of risk management.

☑ Risk database integration is improved when scheduled

Time stays long enough for those who use it.
Leonardo Da Vinci, painter, sculptor, architect, musician,
scientist, mathematician, engineer, inventor, anatomist and geologist

Databases are the work horses of the information age, providing the ability to capture, organise and manage information in a structured and controlled manner. They provide data security, integrity and accuracy. When compared with spreadsheets, they offer greater ease of access, retrieval and sorting.

Key benefits include the ability to carry out simultaneous and concurrent data entry, searches, filtering, printing and viewing. Web-based databases provide yet another dimension to data management by permitting simultaneous data entry from multiple countries across different time zones (see Case Study 26). Ideally, risk databases should be purchased, configured and in use well before the commencement of a major programme or project. For projects with a large number of participating organisations and where each is contributing risk information, risk databases are essential for the efficient implementation of risk management. However, the duration between the time that the decision is made to seek to introduce a risk database to the time that it is fully operational is often underestimated. Risk databases are rarely introduced overnight. As an aside, if the same resource that is assigned to undertake risk management is assigned to organise the procurement and introduction of a risk database, then the risk management processes will suffer.

Database procurement which involves a tender process typically follows a common sequence. The time taken to complete procurement processes which can be undertaken within the risk department can usually be controlled. As soon as it is necessary to involve other departments within the organisation or project, such as information technology, contracts, finance, legal, insurance or business continuity, the degree of control over time management can be diminished. The introduction of a risk database needs to be managed as if it were a project in its own right with a clear understanding of who is doing what and when.

Figure 8.12 illustrates the procurement process similar to that adopted for a web-based project risk database procured for a construction project in Malaysia. The figure is shown as a loop as commonly databases are rarely left unchanged during the life of an organisation.

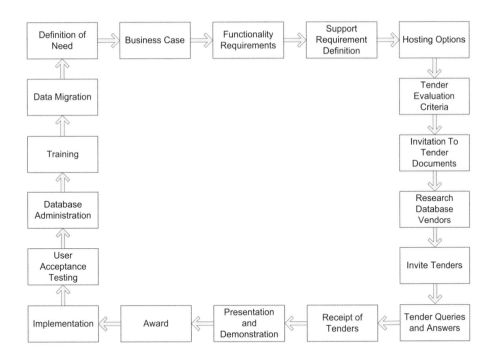

Figure 8.12   Database procurement sequence

Time can be saved by giving early consideration to the following activities which are based on Figure 8.12 above:

- *Funding*: establishing at the outset the source of funding, the budget available and the likely outturn cost. Determine the tax payments to be paid, such as VAT in the UK or local taxes in say Asian countries.

- *Resource-loaded programme*: preparing, agreeing and disseminating a programme for the procurement process at the outset. Recording who will be responsible for each activity. Establishing the activities that are to be undertaken in parallel, overlapped or implemented sequentially.

- *Vendor shortlist*: obtaining approval for the vendors to be invited to tender well in advance of the tender issue date.

- *Functionality*: preparing a schedule of the required functionality of the software relating to, for example: simulation, sensitivity analysis, correlation, distributions, file structure, risk scales, reporting, data security, hyperlinks to external records, email reminders, importing/exporting data to Microsoft files, user administration, simultaneous data entry, compliance with ISO 31000, user administration, probability and impact scales, trend analysis, full text search, automated sequential numbering, adding prefixes and suffixes to risk identification numbers, multi-site operation, risk library and multiple risk categories.

- *Administration*: the creation of role types (such as administrator, risk manager, team member, contractor, etc.) and assignment of role characteristics (what can be viewed, added, changed, etc.), together with the creation of folders and report types.

- *Licences*: establishing the number of licences required and their grouping.

- *Training requirements*: the training requirements to be provided by the vendor will be a function of the funds available for initial and follow-up training over the life of the project, the number of initial and subsequent licences that will be purchased, whether project offices are widely dispersed and whether risk personnel should receive "train-the-trainer" instruction to provide ongoing support to the project.

- *Internal approvals*: establishing what approvals are required from whom and what information they will expect to see in order to make a decision.

- *Maintenance*: establishing ongoing maintenance requirements, such as a help desk, patches, etc.

- *Hosting*: determining early on in the programme the implications of internal hosting, such as costs, server(s) required, licence(s) required, location, security arrangements, business continuity provisions, disaster recovery, back-up power supplies, procurement times and Internet speeds (for web-based tools).

- *Tender evaluation criteria*: establishing the tender evaluation criteria in a timely manner. The criteria should be based on the functionality, hosting and maintenance requirements that have been described separately.

- *Contract preparation*: obtaining (where possible) templates previously used for the procurement of other software involving the stipulation of the functionality, evaluation, training schedule, implementation sequence and hosting requirements. Commencing the preparation of the contract in advance so that the contract terms can be discussed and agreed with the IT, legal, insurance and contracts departments in a timely manner.

- *Presentation and demonstration*: it is prudent to call the tenderers in one at a time following the receipt of tenders so that they can explain how their product meets the functionality requirements, hosting arrangements, planned implementation, training and ongoing maintenance and support.

- *Implementation*: a programme needs to be established for the period following installation up to the stage where the software is operational.

- *User acceptance tests*: tests need to be carried out post-implementation to ensure that the software functions as stipulated in the functional requirements.

- *Database administration*: establishing who will have access to the database (i.e. who will be named users) and specifically who will have access to which folders within the database. Once this has been agreed, the database needs to be configured accordingly to provide the required level of data security.

- *Data migration*: determining what current data has to be migrated and the quickest and simplest way of transferring the spreadsheet information into the database without compromising the integrity of the data. Clearly, the longer it takes to introduce a database into a project, the greater the volume of data that has to be migrated and hence the greater the challenge to get this accomplished quickly.

An example of a project where a web-based project risk database was adopted is described in Case Study 26 below. At the time of the decision being made to acquire a database, the project package strategy had been agreed, construction and railway systems contract documents had been prepared (or were under preparation) and tendering had commenced. The common benefits of a database were sought particularly in light of the geographical dispersion of the project (rail projects are linear) and the international spread of contractors' "home" offices (headquarters).

CASE STUDY 26 – SUNGAI BULOH-KAJANG LINE, KUALA LUMPUR, MALAYSIA

The developer and asset owner of this project is the Mass Rapid Transit Corporation Sdn Bhd (MRT Corp), which is fully owned by the Ministry of Finance. The first Klang Valley Mass Rapid Transit line approved for implementation is the Sungai Buloh-Kajang railway line, which is 51 km long. The line starts at Sungai Buloh, which is located to the north-west of Kuala Lumpur, runs through the city centre of Kuala Lumpur and ends in Kajang. The line will serve a corridor with an estimated population of 1.2 million people. The line will be elevated for a distance of 41.5 km and underground for the remaining 9.5 km, and will be served by 31 stations. The planned operational date of Phase 1 (Sungai Buloh to Semantan) is December 2016, while that of Phase 2 (Semantan to Kajang) is July 2017. Each train serving the line will have four coaches, giving a total capacity of 1,200 passengers. The daily expected ridership will be about 400,000 passengers. The Underground Works (UGW) are being completed as a design-and-build (D&B) contract. The elevated works, depots and railway systems are being delivered by a project delivery partner (PDP). Both the UGW D&B contractor and the PDP appointed by MRT Corp have risk management responsibilities. The PDP is responsible for the advance works plus eight elevated works contracts, two depot contracts and 12 railway systems contracts, giving a total of 22 works package contractors (WPCs). Each of the 22 WPCs has a contractual requirement to perform specific risk management duties. A prerequisite then for the PDP risk management process was to capture and report on risk management information from 22 contracting organisations, the PDP's own management, MRT Corp and the UGW D&B contractor. While capturing and aggregating information from conventional spreadsheets would not have been impossible, it would have been very time-consuming. The decision was taken to procure a web-based PRM database expeditiously to capture and report risk information. The "Active Risk Manager" database supplied by Active Risk Limited of the UK (the vendor) was selected. To follow project processes and seek value for money, the database was procured through a formal tender process. Risk process familiarisation, software configuration and train-the-trainer software training was undertaken by the software vendor. The overall shortlisting, tender preparation, appointment, implementation process and project staff training were undertaken sequentially. The database was used by WPCs based in Japan, France, Singapore, Thailand, Germany and Malaysia. The overall procurement process to the point that the database was "live" took just over five months.

Recognise the time required to introduce a risk database.

☑ Risk model results are improved by sense checking

When models turn on, brains turn off.

Til Schuermann, Partner,

Oliver Wyman, global management consultancy

There are now sophisticated software tools and computers with high processor speeds[29] for carrying out simulations to to make predictions about the outturn cost or duration of a project or programme. However, the reliance that can be placed on these simulation results largely depends on the quality of the inputs. The risk for project sponsors is that they decide to base funding application decisions on outturn cost and duration predictions derived from risk simulation results that have not been vigorously reviewed. Project sponsors together with project and risk managers have to be wary of garbage in, garbage out. Garbage in, garbage out[30] (commonly abbreviated to the acronym GIGO) is a phrase used in the fields of computer science as well as information and communication technology. The term found common appeal in the early days of computing, but is of even greater significance today, due to the ever-growing dependency on increasingly sophisticated computer software. It is commonly used to describe failures in human decision making due to faulty, incomplete or imprecise data. In simple language, it is used to call attention to the fact that computers that are fed poor-quality input data ("garbage in") will as a consequence produce poor-quality output ("garbage out"). For any data analysis processes reliant on software applications, the quality of the underlying

---

29 A computer's speed depends primarily on how fast the central processing unit (CPU) is and how much random access memory (RAM) the computer has. More RAM will allow a computer to store more temporary information, thereby speeding it up.

30 The first use of the term is thought to be on 1 April 1963, when it was referred to in a syndicated newspaper article about the first stages of the computerisation of the US Internal Revenue Service.

data is crucial. Inadequately compiled inputs and correspondingly suspect outputs leave recipients running the risk of drawing the wrong conclusions and making decisions on false assumptions. The most obvious example is the use of risk information presented to boards of banks in the global financial crisis, the impact of which is still being felt today.[31]

The behaviour of the banking sector gave weight to more recent permutation of the GIGO acronym-"garbage in–gospel out". It is a critical and derisive comment on the tendency to put excessive trust in "computerised" data and to blindly accept the simulation output results. Since the data goes through a computer, the mindset is to believe it. In addition, decision makers faced computer-generated information and analyses that could not be collected and analysed in any other way. Precisely for that reason, independently checking the results without the use of computers was out of the question, even if they had good cause to be doubtful about the results. In short, the computer analysis becomes gospel. During the financial crisis, statistical and mathematical sophistication ended up not containing risk, but providing false assurance that the emerging risks could be safely ignored.

For PRM, it is prudent to review how the risk model[32] was constructed (the inputs) and how the simulation was conducted (i.e. the settings selected on the software). Listed below are some of the common problem areas. There is no substitution for experience. The degree to which these aspects of modelling will be prevalent will be related to the experience of the individual

---

31   There are many lessons to be learned from the financial crisis. There is a considerable body of opinion that considers that poor risk management lay at the heart of the credit crisis. This lack of awareness of risk exposure was reinforced by Sir John Gieve (the then Deputy Governor of the Bank of England), who stated that a weakness in the British banking system "was the failure of the banks and many other investors to appreciate, price and manage risk". Bank CEOs took comfort from the sophistication of their risk management systems and hedging strategies, and were confident they could ride out the storm. The issue though was that the bank's systems were preparing them for a shower, not a hurricane. The predominant assumption of the banks was that the scale and complexity of the securitised credit market had been matched by the evolution of statistically sophisticated and effective techniques for measuring and managing the resulting risks. Central to many of the techniques applied was the concept of Value-at-Risk (VAR), enabling mathematical inferences about forward-looking risk (and future price movements) to be drawn from the observation of past patterns of price movement. However, the financial crisis has revealed severe problems with these techniques. Commentators suggest at the very least the need for significant changes in the way that VAR-based methodologies have been applied: nevertheless, some pose more fundamental questions about our ability in principle to infer future risk from patterns observed in the past.

32   The term "model" here is used to describe a representation of reality. A model is usually created using a Microsoft Excel workbook containing multiple worksheets. Simulation is carried out using proprietary "commercially-off-the-shelf" software, which is an add-on to Microsoft Excel.

constructing the model, combined with the degree of diligence the project team exercised in compiling the risks and their characteristics:

- *Unrepresentative assessment of the characteristics of threats and opportunities*: this may include an overly optimistic (or pessimistic) assessment of the probabilities and the impacts[33] and/or an overly optimistic assessment of opportunities (the values assigned to the opportunities would not be borne out in reality).

- *Inadequate articulation of the risk relationships*: this may lead to a lack of recognition of the relationship between risks, such as whether the risks will occur sequentially (in series) or in parallel (for instance, a number of parallel risks impacting a single activity may be "absorbed" within the risk with the greatest time impact) or the inclusion of a correlation between related risks being omitted.

- *Incomplete identification of the threats and opportunities*: there are a number of factors which may contribute to incomplete identification, such as: the speed at which the risk identification and analysis process was undertaken; not all of the project disciplines being represented at brainstorming sessions; the output from previous lessons learned exercises not being drawn upon; the use of checklists resulting in the unique characteristics of the project being overlooked; senior staff and project managers sending inexperienced staff to risk meetings; and a lack of appreciation or examination of the project context.

- *Model construction errors*: there are a number of pitfalls in constructing computer models. There may be errors in formulae, formulae pulling information from the wrong cells horizontally, summation cells not including information from all of the relevant risks vertically (individual risks while captured in the risk register, mistakenly omitted from the simulation), a lack of appreciation that a risk may impact multiple project activities on the programme simultaneously rather than just one and/or the omission of very

---

33 For instance, on a construction project, a risk analysis does not recognise that a risk will lead not only to additional design costs but also to additional local authority fees, construction rework costs and the payment of contractor preliminaries.

low-probability but very high-impact risks due to their significant impact on and perceived "distortion" of the results.

- *Duplication of risks*: a common error in risk evaluation is to double-count risks. This error can occur in a number of ways. It may occur when different members of the project team identify the same risk but describe it in a dissimilar way such that on cursory inspection (and without constructive challenge), the risks appear different.

- *Frequency*: a lack of recognition that the risk is likely to happen more than once during the life of the project – what might be called the frequency of the risk.

A project risk team in the Middle East hastily submitted the output of a simulation to its client for the purpose of setting contingencies without checking it for sense. There had been no comparison of the risk figure with the capital value or the project duration. The risk management process was discredited and the client lost all confidence in simulation outputs. So, for instance, if a project is in its infancy (when there is typically considerable uncertainty), is complex in nature, has a high capital value and involves novel technology, then the risk exposure is likely to be high. However, if this same project is situated in a hostile environment, will have to rely on a complex supply chain and is expected to be executed over many years, then the initial risk exposure might be expected to be very high. So, if the results of the simulation show the aggregate risk exposure is, for example, only one per cent of the capital value, the figure should sound a warning klaxon that the model composition is highly unlikely to be a true representation of the actual risk exposure.

Sense check inputs to and outputs from a risk model before recommending the results are adopted for setting contingencies.

☑ Risk management is enhanced through integration

Project risk management does not exist in a vacuum, isolated from other project management processes.

PMI (2009) Practice Standard for Project Risk Management.
Newtown Square: Project Management Institute Inc., US

For a project to be successful, risk management needs to be integrated with the other project disciplines and processes throughout the PLC from inception through to commissioning and handover. All too often, risk management is introduced late in the project life cycle. By then, key decisions have already been made. As a result, opportunities to derive the potential benefits of risk management have been significantly diluted. Included in Figure 8.13 below are a number of areas of project delivery where risk management should be fully integrated:

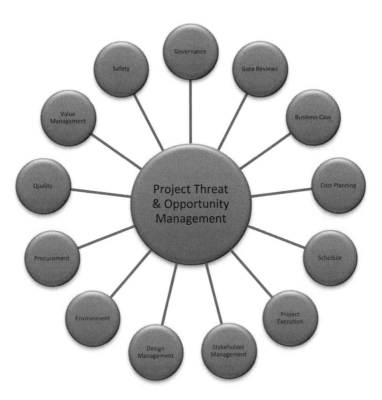

Figure 8.13   Integration of risk management with other project disciplines

- *Governance*: be integral with project governance whereby the organisational structure, responsibility matrix and job descriptions appropriately reflect the project scope. Governance includes change control and the expenditure of contingencies. For contingencies to be defined, the discipline must be integrated with cost planning and scheduling to provide robust and realistic defendable contingencies for cost and time respectively.

- *Gate reviews*: risk management should form an integral part of stage gate reviews, which are an important subset of overall governance. The stage gate review process examines projects at key decision points in their life cycle. It looks ahead to provide assurance that a project can progress successfully to the next stage or recommends additional work be undertaken prior to progression. Gate reviews are a safeguard for the sponsor. They discern whether the original business case is being satisfied and whether further funding should be committed to the project. Reviews are undertaken by review teams who investigate pre-determined topics for evidence that the required activities for the PLC stage under examination have been satisfactorily completed.

- *Business case*: risk management should support the development of a business case involving the analysis and comparison of alternative feasibility options to aid the selection of the preferred option. The comparison of the options should take cognisance of the risk exposure profile of each alternative solution. These profiles may vary considerably.

- *Cost planning*: risk management can be used to determine the cost uncertainty in the cost plan and aid validation of the contingency or be used as the basis for the contingency determination. In addition, risk management should be integrated with change management which might be considered as a subset of cost planning. The discipline should ideally be a formal part of the change control process so that there is an understanding of how the planned change(s) will affect the overall risk exposure of the project.

- *Schedule*: the schedule should be used to guide the prioritisation of risk management activity, to judge the appropriate scale of risk impacts, to understand the relationship between risks (i.e.

if they would occur in parallel or series) and to consider the appropriateness of periods of float built into the programme. Risk management should focus on the key threats to the critical path.

- *Project execution*: risk management needs to be implemented throughout the PLC and hence this should include project execution/ construction. As a consequence, tender documents should stipulate the contractor's risk obligations. This may include the provision of a risk register with their tender which clearly indicates who they believe will be the owner of each risk and the likely range of the risk impact should it materialise. They may be reticent to include potential opportunities in their tender for fear that they would be shared with another bidder. Depending on the type of contract, the tender documents may stipulate that the contractor has to submit a risk management plan, update a risk register at least monthly and attend monthly risk management meetings.

- *Stakeholder management*: as part of the context stage of the risk management process, gaining an appreciation of who the primary stakeholders are and their degree of influence on the project outcomes will be significant in gaining an understanding of the potential sources of threat. At the outset, the stakeholders will be instrumental in determining the project objectives, scope, sponsorship, boundaries, key constraints and assumptions. Involving a primary stakeholder such as an end user or operator late in the process can result in scope changes, cost increases, an extension to the programme and an erosion of reputation.

- *Design management*: design management can be the source of threats to the project objectives in terms of the timing of the production of the design, the degree of completeness of the design, the satisfactory incorporation of the project scope in the design and the degree of success of the integration of the disparate design disciplines.

- *Environment*: the time taken to obtain environmental approvals together with the imposition of approval conditions and monitoring requirements by authorities can lead to very significant constraints being placed on project delivery. When unexpected delays occur during the approval process, projects can be exposed to considerable uncertainty.

- *Procurement*: risk management has a vital role to play in the selection of the procurement route, the form of contract, the contract conditions and the tendering process. The decisions made should reflect the project sponsor's risk appetite and the preferred degree of risk transfer. All of the steps in the procurement process are about risk management and risk ownership. Risk management introduced after the type of contract has been selected robs a project of being able to both articulate and manage risk.

- *Quality*: quality can be measured in terms of the design adhering to the project brief, appropriate codes and standards, the operational cost constraints/requirements of clients and compliance of contractors with the scope, drawings, specifications and workmanship requirements. Hence, risk management in this context is where design and/or construction do not comply with pre-determined quality benchmarks and reworking is required.

- *Value management*: risk management should be integrated with the discipline of value management through an understanding of the client's value system and the project's value chain, and recognising that risk exposure is a byproduct of the pursuit of value. Value management is about enhancing value and not about cutting costs, although this may be a side-effect.

- *Health and safety*: the health and safety department on the project may have its own approach to risk and may maintain its own register with a view to minimising injuries and preventing fatalities. However, PRM is concerned with how health and safety incidents may impact on the project objectives (which may be just cost, time and quality or much broader, including reputation and ethics). Risk management is concerned with, for instance, how an incident such as the collapse of temporary works and the injury to construction operatives would impact on the completion date.

Risk management needs to be integrated with the other project disciplines throughout the PLC.

Appendix A:
The EFQM Excellence Model

The European Foundation for Quality Management (EFQM) Excellence Model[1] is the most popular quality tool in Europe and is used by more than 30,000 organisations to improve performance. The EFQM originated 25 years ago in 1988 when 14 CEOs joined forces to develop a management tool that was aimed at increasing the competitiveness of European organisations. Supported by the European Commission in the European Quality Promotion Policy, the Foundation created the EFQM Excellence Model. An illustration of the Model and its nine assessment criteria (as published by the EFQM) is included in Figure A.1. The arrows in the graph represent the dynamic nature of the Model, showing learning, creativity and innovation helping to improve the enablers that in turn lead to improved results.

Through the nine criteria included within the Model, organisations can understand and analyse the cause-and-effect relationships between what an organisation does and the results it achieves. Five of these criteria are "Enablers" and four are "Results". The "Enabler" criteria cover what an organisation does and how it does it. The "Results" criteria cover what an organisation achieves. Each of the nine criteria has a definition, which explains the high-level meaning of each criterion. To develop the high-level meaning further, each criterion is supported by a number of criterion parts. The nine assessment criteria are: leadership; people; strategy; partnerships and resources; processes, products and services; customer results; people results; society results; and key results.

---

1   EFQM is the custodian of the business model called the EFQM Excellence Model. It is a global not-for-profit membership foundation based in Brussels. It declares that it has more than 500 members covering more than 55 countries and 50 industries, and provides a unique platform for organisations to learn from each other and improve performance.

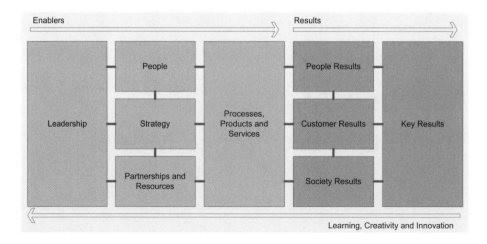

Figure A.1   EFQM Excellence Model

For the discipline of project risk management, a simplified model is proposed here which was used in broad terms and not prescriptively to guide the structure of this book. The revised model is illustrated in Figure A.2 and was influenced by the UK HM Treasury assessment framework.[2] This model has seven assessment criteria: project risk management leadership; resources; organisation; stakeholders (such as contractors and suppliers); project risk management processes; risk management effectiveness; and outcomes. The first five criteria are classed as "enablers" and the remaining two are classed as "results".

---

2   HM Treasury (2009) "Risk Management Assessment Framework: A Tool for Departments", https://www.gov.uk/government/uploads/system/uploads/attachment_data/file/191516/Risk_ management_assessment_framework.pdf.

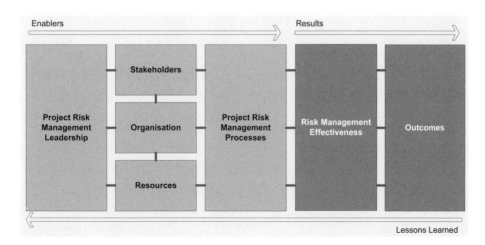

Figure A.2   Risk management model

Appendix B: Systems Thinking[1]

The Appeal of Systems Thinking

The appeal of systems thinking to the modelling of the design process within major construction projects arises from its focus on the interrelationships of the component parts and their influence upon the effectiveness of the total process. This approach is particularly relevant to the design process as its success depends to a large extent upon the way in which the contributors – the project manager, architect, geotechnical engineer, structural engineer, mechanical engineer, landscape architect and commonly several other disciplines – work together. What each of them achieves depends upon what the others do. They are totally reliant upon each other for the satisfactory completion of a project, for design development is dependent on the quality and extent of the integration of these highly differentiated skills. In organisations which are strongly differentiated yet largely interdependent, such as those often involved in construction projects, the key to success is the quality and extent of the integrative effort provided by the discipline leaders of the project team. At a basic level, the discipline leader will need to ensure that the appropriate people with the right skills are involved at the correct time. Walker states that "this may be obvious but is still surprising how little this does happen".[2] Pokora and Hastings provide a clear insight into the ramifications of specialisation which directly reflects on the degree and difficulty of integration: "the characteristic of specialists is that they are chiefly interested in technicalities and contribute on this restricted front ... they will not necessarily see the 'big picture'".[3] If advice is given too late in the process or if it is not given at all or not taken, it can lead to abortive work or delay and to client dissatisfaction with the

---

1 The following are extracts from Chapman, R.J. (1998) "The Role of Systems Dynamics in Understanding the Impact of Changes to Key Project Personnel on Design Production within Construction Projects", *International Journal of Project Management*, 16(4), 235–47.
2 Walker, A. (1984) *Project Management in Construction*. London: Granada Publishing.
3 Pokara, J. and Hastings, C. (1995) "Building Partnerships: Teamworking and Alliances in the Construction Industry", Construction Paper, No. 54, Chartered Institute of Building.

outcome of the project. Definitions of a system abound, but they all have a common theme – they describe elements that function together for a common objective. Morris describes a system as "an assemblage of people, things, information, organisations etc. grouped together according to a particular system objective".[4] Ackoff[5] describes a system as "any entity, conceptual or physical, which consists of interdependent parts. Each of a system's elements is connected to every other element, directly or indirectly, and no sub-set of elements is unrelated to any other sub-set". Perhaps the simplest and most concise description is that offered by Roberts et al., who state that "a system may be defined as a collection of interacting elements that function together for some purpose".[6]

The motives to apply system dynamics proposed by Rodrigues et al. would appear to be common and are adopted here:

- a concern to consider the whole project rather than a sum of the individual elements (the holistic approach);

- the need to examine major non-linear aspects typically described by balancing or reinforcing feedback loops;

- a need for a flexible project model which offers a laboratory for experiments with management options; and

- the failure of traditional analytic tools to solve all project management problems and the desire to experiment with something new.

The Systems Dynamic Approach

System dynamics is concerned with creating models or representations of real-world systems of all kinds and studying their dynamics (or behaviour). In particular, it is concerned with improving (controlling) problematic system behaviour. The purpose of applying system dynamics is to facilitate an understanding of the relationship between the behaviour of a system *over time*

4   Morris, P.W.G. (1983) "Project Management Organisation", *CIOB Construction Papers*, 2(1).
5   Ackoff, R.L. (1969) "Systems, Organisation and Interdisciplinary Research" in F.E. Emery (ed.), *Systems Thinking*. London: Penguin.
6   Roberts, N. et al. (1983) *Introduction to Computer Simulation: The System Dynamics Approach*. Reading, MA: Addison-Wesley.

and its underlying structure and decision rules.[7] The use of system dynamics causal-loop diagrams to structure, analyse and communicate ill-defined situations can be considered as a free-standing methodology, having much in common with the soft system problem-solving approaches of Checkland and Ackoff. This type of medium is useful because it provides a less ambiguous and more condensed form of communication than a written description.

The Evolution of General Systems Theory and System Dynamics

System science emerged as a serious field of study after the Second World War. Originally the field was rooted in biological and engineering sciences, only more recently branching out to become more involved with social economic problems. General systems theory (GST) developed from the view that there existed general system laws which apply to any system of a certain type, irrespective of the particular properties of the system and of the elements involved.[8] It grew out of research in a number of disciplines, which include Shannon and Weaver's work in information theory,[9] Ashby's model for adaptiveness[10] and Wiener's cybernetics,[11] which all looked at concepts of entropy (disorder), feedback and interaction between components. However, it was von Bertalanffy who insisted that the emerging ideas in the various fields could be generalised into systems thinking and in consequence is recognised as the movement's founder.[12] Of interest here is Wiener's cybernetics, one of the scientific developments embraced by systems theory, which acted as a catalyst for what was to become known as system dynamics. Cybernetics appeared in 1948 and was the result of the then-recent developments of computer technology, information theory and self-regulating machines. Wiener carried the cybernetic, feedback and information concepts far beyond the fields of technology and generalised it in the biological and social realms. It was Forrester who applied the broad principles of cybernetics to systems in an industrial setting in his book *Industrial Systems.*[13] Forrester's initial work has subsequently been broadened by Wolstenholme to include other social,

7   Wolstenholme, E.F. (1990) *System Enquiry: A System Dynamics Approach.* Chichester: John Wiley and Sons.
8   Von Bertalanffy, L. (1968) *General System Theory: Foundation Development Applications.* New York: George Braziller Inc.
9   Shannon C.E. and Weaver, W. (1949) *The Mathematical Theory of Communication.* Urbana: University of Illinois Press.
10 Ashby, R.W. (1956) *Introduction to Cybernetics.* London: Chapman & Hall.
11 Wiener, N. (1948) *Cybernetics.* New York: Wiley.
12 Checkland, P. (1981) *Systems Thinking, Systems Practice.* Chichester: John Wiley & Sons.
13 Forrester, J.W. (1961) *Industrial Dynamics.* Cambridge, MA: MIT Press.

economic and environmental systems, and is now known as the field of system dynamics. The first description of the use of system dynamics appeared in 1964, but it was not until the 1980s that the first project-specific applications began to be reported. Through the study of research and development (R&D) and software projects, developments in system dynamics have taken place to model evolving problem areas, resulting in the introduction of new concepts. The field of system dynamics is one of several possible variants of the system approach.[14]

---

14 Meadows, D.H. (1972) *Limits to Growth*. New York: Universe Books.

Appendix C:
Causes of Project Failure

Table C.1   *Gateway Lessons Learned Key Themes 2010/2011* (published by the UK Department of Finance and Personnel: http://www. dfpni.gov.uk)

Key Area	Key Lesson	Sub Lessons
Business Case	The business case is a dynamic document which should reflect the updated strategic context and be regularly reviewed.	There should be a programme business case even where project business cases exist as this will inform business process change and objective challenge, and provide a test for programme-level assumptions.
Change	A clear policy framework will increase and enhance the effectiveness of service delivery and aid business change.	It is important to focus on incremental change to the accrual of benefit, using an annual business improvement plan to avoid the temptation to step change.
Procurement	A detailed procurement strategy which articulates an understanding of the supplier market capacity, the grounds for selecting the preferred route and providing a clear policy for future procurement will inform VFM.	Roles and responsibilities of the evaluation panel members should be clearly defined, together with the role of CPD in all relevant documentation.
		Where a non-standard procurement route is being considered, use should be made of techniques such as benchmarking to ensure that value for money can be demonstrated.
	Contract management arrangements should be put in place as soon as the business case is approved.	The project team should ensure that there is a clear separation of roles where an incumbent supplier is bidding for a future contract. It is important that the integrity of the contract negotiations is not compromised.

Table C.1   *Gateway Lessons Learned Key Themes 2010/2011* (published by the UK Department of Finance and Personnel: http://www. dfpni.gov.uk) *continued*

Key Area	Key Lesson	Sub Lessons
Programme and Project Management (based on the themes of 2009/2010**)**	Both programmes and projects need to employ appropriate methodologies, governance structures and skills to ALL elements to provide assurance for the delivery of the overall objectives.	Links between individual projects should be streamlined to ensure they fully integrate with the overall programme.
		Where the programme is high profile and has a variety of projects, an independent nonexec director should be considered for the programme board to provide a challenge function across all aspects of the programme to ensure effective delivery.
		When two programmes progress in parallel rather than as an integral whole there will be a considerable amount of overlap and duplication between them. The reasons may arise from different accountabilities, however once implementation begins it would be helpful for a more unified portfolio/programme management structure to be adopted.
		Stakeholder representation within the programme/ project management structure is key to the successful delivery of benefits and transition to the new service.
Planning (based on the themes of 2009/2010)	Plans should be realistic and achievable and address all elements of the programme/ project from the earliest possible stages; they are also subject to regular review to ensure current, relevant content is available.	A high level integrated project and resource plan supported by more detailed stage plans with specific objectives is required to proactively plan and manage the next phases of the project to ensure that quality outputs are produced on time and to budget.
		Robust contingency plans which can be applied quickly are required to minimise delays or slippage in the programme/project.
		A project can lose sight of its purpose if plans for benefits realisation are left too late.
		The preparation of a plan should not be seen as the end of a project, which is a continuum of activity progressing from the planning phase to readiness and finally to delivery.
		A handover plan that identified "post go live" services and formally assigns responsibilities and resources will provide assurance of successful delivery and subsequent management.

Table C.1   *Gateway Lessons Learned Key Themes 2010/2011* (published by the UK Department of Finance and Personnel: http://www. dfpni.gov.uk) *continued*

Key Area	Key Lesson	Sub Lessons
		Resourcing assumptions should be revisited regularly as the programme/project moves forward.
		A fully resourced project plan should be prepared to take account of performance management and progress reporting and needs to identify the critical path, highlighting key milestones and the interdependency of key activities.
		Adequate skilled project and contract management resources are vital to the success of a project
		Service Management resourcing should have clear roles and responsibilities and document support procedures to ensure all parties understand their respective responsibilities.
Benefits	Clearly owned, agreed and measured benefits, concentrated on the business and end users, are essential for all programmes and projects. Early collection of baseline data with a detailed delivery plan and clearly identified and dated realisation activities are required to prevent a project losing sight of its purpose.	All benefits should be consolidated into a single benefits management plan that details in a clear way how benefits will be measured, appropriate ownership and show progress against the measures.
Governance	Formal governance structures should be defined at the outset of the programme or project with terms of reference to ensure continued effective management of the programme or project going forward.	Governance and management disciplines should be applied routinely to all aspects of the programme or project. This will ensure critical risks and issues are highlighted to the board early, plans are tested regularly and strategic leadership, guidance and challenge is effective.
		Governance includes management boards and these should consist of a minimum number of members to enable effective decision making and strategic focus with key stakeholders represented.
		Where appropriate governance can include a number of boards, such as stakeholder/sponsor board, programme board and project board, each should have clear terms of reference and reporting/decision making documented and communicated.
Stakeholders	Stakeholders can impact or influence the success of any change programme or project.	All project stakeholders should have a clear understanding of the major risks and how they are being addressed.

Table C.1   *Gateway Lessons Learned Key Themes 2010/2011* (published by the UK Department of Finance and Personnel: http://www. dfpni.gov.uk) *continued*

Key Area	Key Lesson	Sub Lessons
		SRO should ensure that the consultation and communication strategy is reviewed and updated to frame and support stakeholder engagement activities as the project progresses.
		All stakeholder organisations should be clear in their understanding of the elements of the programme that relate to their own organisational objectives.
		A stakeholder map and management plan should be generated to underpin consultation processes within projects.
Risk	Individual risk owners should be recorded for each identified risk.	A risk register should exist that allocates specific ownership to identified risks. Multiple members of the team should not be identified as risk owners of single risks – this is not good practice.
		Risk registers should not be prepared just ahead of the Review – they should be comprehensive and an integral part of the project management process. Risks should be owned by individuals rather than by organisations. This supports better risk control, review and escalation.
	A comprehensive and proactive risk management strategy, including an up to date risk register, must be in place.	A single, integrated risk register should be produced and maintained for the remainder of the project.
		There should be a formal and appropriate risk management process in place for the overall project. Risk registers should be produced in a workshop setting involving key stakeholders. Registers need to be kept up to date with identified risk mitigation actions carried out and recorded.
		Risk registers should contain an articulation of identified risk which are programme/project-specific. Top priority project risks should be captured and escalated to the programme level and communicated to the programme manager as necessary.
		For works/construction projects, a schedule for the non-construction elements of the project must be drawn up. This should be publicised and maintained. A proactive, simple risk reporting regime should be introduced to support the current risk management arrangements.

Table C.1   *Gateway Lessons Learned Key Themes 2010/2011* (published by the UK Department of Finance and Personnel: http://www. dfpni.gov.uk) *continued*

Key Area	Key Lesson	Sub Lessons
		All risks should be identified within the risk register. A risk management strategy that includes processes for report and escalation of risks and linkage to overall organisational risk management strategy should be produced. Sufficient detail on how risks are dealt with by the project board should be recorded.
		A comprehensive, overall, project-specific risk register covering the full range of risks affecting the project should be produced. The focus should not just be on cost – risks need to be prioritised.
	Issues should be managed appropriately and distinguished from risks.	An issue log should be developed alongside the project risk register. Issues should be differentiated from risks and recorded appropriately.
		The issues log should be more focussed on issues with significant impact on project delivery. Assistance with this can be obtained from the PMO.
Roles and Responsibilities	A project specific succession plan to cover the duration of the project should be produced.	This will ensure that the correct calibre of staff are recruited and trained to replace staff who are moving on.
		It is especially important for key posts such as Project Sponsor, Senior Responsible Owner and project manager.
	Lack of clearly defined and agreed roles and responsibilities throughout the programme or project life cycle will lead to confusion, lack of ownership and adversarial relationships, which will put successful delivery seriously at risk.	The role and responsibilities of the project manager must be clearly defined, agreed and communicated to avoid any confusion between that role and a project manager involved with one aspect of the project.
		A lack of clearly defined roles will lead to confusion within the stakeholder community about the governance of the project or programme.
		Once a significant role is defined, it is imperative to the success of the project or programme that the resource is assigned on a full-time basis.

Table C.1   *Gateway Lessons Learned Key Themes 2010/2011* (published
by the UK Department of Finance and Personnel: http://www.
dfpni.gov.uk) *concluded*

Key Area	Key Lesson	Sub Lessons
Communications	Stakeholder communication strategies and plans should be revisited at regular intervals.	Programmes and projects should revisit their strategies and plans regularly. This provides the opportunity to clearly articulate and communicate with all stakeholders the benefits that have already been delivered. It also allows the reinforcement of their strategic partnerships.
		Regular review of the communication strategy and plan will ensure that there continues to be two-way engagement with both the internal and external stakeholders.
Configuration Management	All programme and project close criteria should be clearly documented.	
	Programmes and projects must have clear and concise policies on version control for key documentation.	Poor version control risks ill-informed decision making.
Resourcing	Clear forecasting and monitoring of a project's budgets will lead to improved financial control within the project	
	Good human resource planning will assist in the retention and recruitment of necessary staff to ensure the success of the programme or project.	Poor resource planning can lead to existing staff becoming frustrated and stressed. It can also be a block to the recruitment of suitable new staff.

Note: VFM = value for money; CPD = Central Procurement Directorate; PMO = Program Management Office; SRO = Senior Responsible Owner.

Table C.2   OGC common causes of project failure (published by the UK Office of Government Commerce (OGC), an Office of HM Treasury, in 2005)

No	Common causes of project failure
1	Lack of clear links between the project and the organisation's key strategic priorities (including agreed measures of success).
2	Lack of senior management and Ministerial ownership and leadership.
3	Lack of effective engagement with stakeholders.
4	Lack of skills and proven approach to project and *risk management*.
5	Too little attention to breaking development and implementation into manageable steps.
6	Evaluation of proposals driven by initial price rather than long-term value for money (especially securing delivery of business benefits).
7	Lack of understanding of and contact with the supply industry at senior levels in the organisation.
8	Lack of effective project team integration between clients, the supplier and the supply chain.

Note 1: Within the explanatory notes, it states that the list of common causes of project failure has been agreed between the National Audit Office (NAO) and the OGC.

Note 2: These same causes of project failure were referred to in full (and unchanged) in the OGC Best Management Practice publication "Addressing Project Failure through Prince2™", written by consultant Kenn Dolan and published in August 2010 (http://www.harrybakerprofessionals.com/new/images/articles/Addressing_Project_Failure_through_PRINCE21.pdf).

Table C.3   PRINCE2 common causes of project failure (described in *Managing Successful Projects with PRINCE2*, published by The Stationery Office on behalf of the OGC in 2005)

No	Common causes of project failure
1	Insufficient attention to checking that a valid Business Case exists for the project.
2	Insufficient attention to quality at the outset and during development.
3	Insufficient definition of the required outcomes, leading to confusion over what the project is expected to achieve.
4	Lack of communication with stakeholders and interested parties, leading to products being delivered that are not what the customer wanted.
5	Inadequate definition and lack of acceptance of project management roles and responsibilities, leading to lack of direction and poor decision making.
6	Poor estimation of duration and costs, leading to projects taking more time and costing more money than expected.
7	Inadequate planning and coordination of resources, leading to poor scheduling.
8	Insufficient measurables and lack of control over progress, so that projects do not reveal their exact status until too late.
9	Lack of quality control, resulting in the delivery of products that are unacceptable or unsuitable.

Appendix D:
Observations on the Standard

While the ISO 31000 Standard is highly structured, distilling from it the drivers for effective PRM is not straightforward. It could be argued that the principles or framework are not a natural starting point. It looks as if the Standard is starting "from the inside out". The Standard itself implies a different sequence from the one illustrated. Included below are four bullet points that offer suggestions on the restructuring of ISO 31000 so that the sequence of the subjects rose are ordered more logically:

- The Standard states under the heading "Framework (and the sub-heading "General") that: "If an organisation's existing management practices and processes include components of risk management or if the organisation has already adopted a formal risk management process for particular types of risk or situations, then these should be critically reviewed and assessed against this International Standard … in order to determine their adequacy and effectiveness." It could be argued that any appraisal of existing competencies should be discussed in the introduction prior to the section on the framework, as the framework should reflect the current and desired risk maturity of the organisation or project under examination.

- The Standard states under the heading "Design of framework for managing risk" that: "Before starting on the design and implementation of the framework for managing risk, it is important to evaluate and understand both the internal and external context of the organisation, since these can significantly influence the design of the framework." If that is the case, why are these activities described here? Why is the subject of "context" not a separate section included prior to the section entitled "Framework for managing risk"?

- In addition, again under the heading "Design of framework for managing risk", it is not until you reach the internal context that there is a reference to "capabilities", a subset of which is "knowledge". If this is a reference to the risk maturity of the organisation's risk management practices, it reinforces the argument that the document should be restructured and the context should be examined before the framework.

- Under the "Mandate and commitment" step, the Standard states "Define and endorse the risk management policy" as its first sub-heading. This implies that the policy should be defined and agreed at this stage of the framework's development. However, the task of establishing the risk management policy is also described under the next step in the development of the framework entitled "Design of framework for managing risk".

Appendix E:
Drivers for Project Success

Key Lessons

1. Projects that develop from long-term plans and that have robust business cases are likely to be most successful.

2. Strong project governance arrangements mean strong project delivery.

3. The procurement model should be chosen on the basis of project specifics and should rigorously follow established published guidelines.

4. Risk should be transferred appropriately in order to maintain value for money.

5. Careful management of local and environmental impacts assists project delivery.

6. It is important to be open to learning the lessons from previous projects.

Appendix F:
Mitchell, Bradley and Wood's Stakeholder Typology

Within their article "Toward a Theory of Stakeholder Identification and Salience: Defining the Principle of Who and What Really Counts", which describes a theory of stakeholder identification and salience,[1] Mitchell et al. propose a typology[2] of stakeholders in a firm's environment. This classification approach is equally applicable to the projects that are undertaken by firms. The typology is based on one or more of the attributes of power, legitimacy or urgency that in turn can be used to identify different classes of stakeholder. The literature on stakeholders describes a stakeholder with power as one that has the ability to bring about the outcome it desires. It will have the power to not just influence the achievement of a firm's objectives, but to withdraw resources from the firm and prevent a project from being commenced or completed. A legitimate stakeholder is described as one that has a contractual relationship with the firm, legal title to assets or property of the firm and/ or is exposed to risk from the firm's activities as a result of investing in the firm in terms of, for example, capital (financial or human). The authors argue that power and legitimacy are distinct attributes which can exist independently or can combine together. They state that while a stakeholder may have a legitimate claim on a firm, unless it has the power to enforce its will in the (stakeholder) relationship, it cannot achieve its desired outcome. Given the dynamic nature of stakeholder influence, stakeholders that have the urgency attribute are those that claim for immediate attention.

---

1 Mitchell, R.K. Bradley, R.A. and Wood, D.J. (1997) "Toward a Theory of Stakeholder Identification and Salience: Defining the Principle of Who and What Really Counts", *Academy of Management Review*, 22(4), 853–86.
2 Typology refers to a systematic classification of types that have characteristics or traits in common.

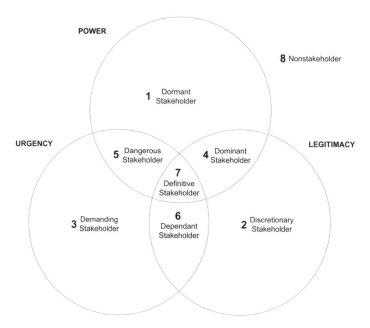

Figure F.1   Stakeholder attributes and classes
Source: Mitchell et al., 1997.

This is particularly important for projects which have specific start and finish dates and typically finite resources. For instance, government agencies, which have to demonstrate value for money when initiating and delivering projects, will call for immediate attention (and action) when delivery deviates from planned progress or pre-agreed milestones. Figure F.1 provides an illustration of the author's stakeholder typology, illustrating both stakeholder attributes and classes.

Mitchell et al. propose that various classes of stakeholders can be identified based on the possession of one, two or all of the attributes. Seven classes are examined. They have given each class a descriptive name to facilitate discussion (see Figure F.1). Dormant stakeholders in principle possess the power to impose their will on a project, but their power remains unused as a result of them having no legitimate relationship or urgent claim. Dormant stakeholders thus have little or no interaction with the project. However, their potential to acquire a second attribute means that risk managers should remain aware of them and their potential impact on the project. Discretionary stakeholders, in turn, possess the attribute of legitimacy, but have no power to influence the project and have no urgent claims. The key point regarding these stakeholders is that, in the absence of power and urgent claims, there is absolutely no pressure on managers to engage in an active relationship with them, although they may well choose to do so (or even ought to do so). Demanding stakeholders have urgent claims, but have no power or legitimacy. When stakeholders are unable or unwilling to move their claim into a position of more significance, protestations of urgency are insufficient to move a stakeholder claim beyond latency. Dormant, discretionary and demanding stakeholders are labelled by Mitchell et al. as latent stakeholders, where stakeholder salience is low. Dominant stakeholders are both powerful and legitimate. Dominant stakeholders commonly have a formal mechanism in play that acknowledges their relationship with the firm. Dangerous stakeholders are characterised by the possession of urgency and power, but they have no legitimacy. Such stakeholders can be coercive and possibly violent, making them, literally, dangerous to the organisation (or project). The actions of these stakeholders can be dangerous to the stakeholder-manager relationship and to the individuals and entities involved. Dependent stakeholders are those that lack power yet have urgent legitimate claims, but an absence of power to carry out their will. Definitive stakeholders are those that already have the attributes of power and legitimacy, but whose claims become urgent. An example is a sponsor who becomes disenchanted by the way his or her project is being run and replaces the project director.

In summary, the article by Mitchell et al. would benefit from further development. For instance, regrettably it offers no case studies to show how the authors' typology could be applied in practice. In addition, the different classes are only briefly described and require further explanation to ensure that they are readily distinguishable from one another.

Appendix G:
The Power/Predictability Matrix

The Power/Predictability Matrix

Figure G.1 illustrates the power/predictability matrix proposed by Aubrey L. Mendelow from Kent State University, Ohio. Zone A stakeholders, who are highly predictable with a low power base, present few problems. Similarly, Zone B stakeholders, who are unpredictable but manageable, are unlikely to introduce significant project uncertainty. Powerful but predictable stakeholders in Zone C, such as lenders, insurance companies and investors in times of low economic growth and prudent measured risk taking, can have a constraining influence on a project's objectives and/or scope. The most difficult stakeholders to manage are Zone D stakeholders, who are unpredictable but powerful. These groups of stakeholders may represent the greatest danger by using their significant power to stop a project in its tracks. An example of contemporary and often controversial projects where the matrix may help to illustrate and communicate the power and predictability of stakeholders, is windfarm developments. The siting of commercial wind farms have been the subject of government intervention. The government has made a commitment to renewable energy targets, while at the same time it is under pressure from conservation groups and the general public not to spoil views of the countryside. The allocation of groups of stakeholders to these zones enables projects to assess the scale of the potential opposition to planned projects. Making decisions which will be acceptable to Zone C stakeholders may influence or overcome resistance from Zone D stakeholders. Although Zone A and B stakeholders have less power, this does not mean that they are unimportant; the support of these stakeholders may have a strong influence on the attitudes of more powerful stakeholders.

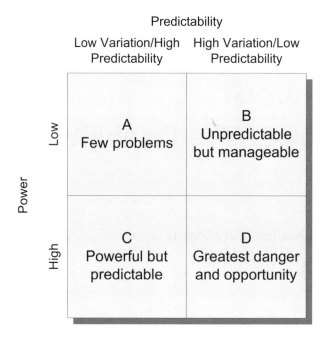

Figure G.1   Predictability/power matrix[1]

The problem with this matrix is the repositioning of stakeholders from Zone C to Zone D. Again, the role of stakeholders in Zones A and B needs to be monitored and controlled because, although lacking in power, they may have a disproportionate influence on the more powerful stakeholders.

Stakeholder management involves classifying stakeholders, as each type of stakeholder will require a different approach to be taken. Clearly, the approach taken in relation to a developer, local authority and community group will need to be very different. Each party has the potential to introduce project uncertainty. The aim of risk management is to reduce that uncertainty. Hence, classification and the definition of the approach must be undertaken early in the project life cycle to facilitate both initial and subsequent engagement with them in a timely, planned and coordinated manner. Some of the broad classifications of stakeholders are listed below, but they offer little assistance in the identification or stakeholders or the determination of response actions:

---

1   Price, D. (2009) *The Principles and Practice of Change*. Basingstoke: Palgrave Macmillan.

- Inside and outside stakeholders.[2]

- Direct and indirect stakeholders.[3]

- Critical and less critical stakeholders.[4]

- Primary and secondary stakeholders.[5]

- Contracted and non-contracted stakeholders.[6]

- Social and non-social stakeholders.[7]

- Internal and external stakeholders.[8]

2   Newcombe, R. (2003) "From Client to Project Stakeholders: A Stakeholder Mapping Approach",
    Construction Management and Economics, 21(8), 841–8.
3   Smith, J. and Love, P.E.D. (2004) "Stakeholder Management During Project Inception: Strategic
    Needs Analysis", *Journal of Architectural Engineering*, 10(1), 22–3.
4   Calvert, S. (1995) *Managing Stakeholders: The Commercial Project Manager*. New York: McGraw-
    Hill.
5   Clarkson, M.B.E. (1995) "A Stakeholder Framework for Analysing and Evaluating Corporate
    Social Performance", *Academy of Management Review*, 20(1), 92–117.
6   Smith and Love (n 3).
7   Carroll, A.B. and Buchholtz, A.K. (2006) *Business and Society: Ethics and Stakeholder Management*,
    6th edn. Mason: Thomson/South-Western.
8   Jeffrey, N. (2009) "Stakeholder Engagement: A Road Map to Meaningful Engagement", https://
    dspace.lib.cranfield.ac.uk/bitstream/1826/3801/3/Stakeholder_engagement-2009.pdf.

Appendix H:
Maturity Model Descriptions

This appendix is to be read in conjunction with the 'rule' that *risk management aspirations need to be rooted in reality*. It describes the Risk Maturity Model levels proposed by the CCTA, Hillson and Hopkinson.

Table H.1   CCTA risk maturity levels[1]

First Level of Maturity
The first type of organisation structure is the "virtual organisation", in which the management of risk is everyone's responsibility. In this situation, it is up to an interested individual manager to pursue good practice in respect of the management of risk.
Second Level of Maturity
The second type of structure is where there is a separate management of risk group consisting of specialists who conduct analyses for operational, project, programme and senior managers. Usually these groups operate on a task-by-task basis, for example, examining a single high-risk project. The usefulness of these groups depends greatly on the talents of the specialists involved and the willingness of individual managers to accept advice.
Third Level of Maturity
The third type of structure exists when the specialist risk group is integrated within existing management groups at each organisational level. More formal mechanisms are needed to communicate risk information among these different groups. Although still mainly task-oriented, more structured or formal management of risk approaches are put in place.
Fourth Level of Maturity
The fourth type of structure is the fully integrated management of risk organisation. In this structure, the management of risk is everyone's responsibility, but formal mechanisms exist to help bring this about. A management of risk infrastructure that incorporates a standard analysis and management process exists.

---

1   CCTA (1993) "Introduction to the Management of Risk", Government Centre for Information Systems, October 1993.

Table H.2   Hillson risk maturity model[2]

Level 1 Naive
The Naive risk organisation is unaware of the need for risk management and has no structured approach for dealing with uncertainty. Management processes are repetitive and reactive, with little or no attempt to learn from the past or to prepare for future threats or uncertainties.
Level 2 Novice
The Novice risk organisation experiments with the application of risk management, usually through a small number of nominated individuals, but has no formal or structured generic process in place. Although aware of the potential benefits of managing risk, the novice organisation has not effectively implemented risk processes and is not gaining the full benefits.
Level 3 Normalised
The Normalised risk organisation has built management of risk into routine business processes and implements risk management on most or all projects. Generic risk processes are formalised and widespread, and the benefits are understood at all levels of the organisation, although they may not be consistently achieved in all cases.
Level 4 Natural
The Natural risk organisation has a risk-aware culture, with a proactive approach to risk management in all aspects of the business. Risk information is actively used to improve business processes and gain competitive advantage. Risk processes are used to manage opportunities as well as potential negative impacts.

Table H.3   Hopkinson risk maturity model[3]

Level 1 Naive
Although a project risk management process may be initiated, its design or application is fundamentally flawed. At this level, it is likely that the process does not add value.
Level 2 Novice
The project risk management process influences decisions taken by the project team in a way that is likely to lead to improvements in project performance as measured against its objectives. However, although the process may add value, weaknesses with either the process design or its implementation result in significant benefits being unrealised.
Level 3 Normalised
The project risk management process is formalised and implemented systematically. Value is added by implementing effective management responses to significant sources of uncertainty that could affect the achievement of the project's objectives.
Level 4 Natural
The risk management process leads to the selection of risk-efficient strategic choices when setting project objectives and choosing between options for project solutions or delivery. Sources of uncertainty that could affect the achievement of project objectives are managed systematically within the context of a team culture that is conducive to optimising project outcomes.

---

2   Hillson, D. (1997) "Towards a Risk Maturity Model", *International Journal of Project and Business Risk Management*, 1(1), 34–45.

3   Hopkinson, M. (2011) *The Project Risk Maturity Model: Measuring and Improving Risk Management Capability*. Farnham: Gower.

Appendix I:
Recording Lessons Learned

A possible format for capturing lessons learned is contained in Table I.1.

Table I.1   Lessons learned

Sponsor:	
Project Name:	
Project Manager:	
Identify which project management disciplines were involved.	
State the procurement route, form of contract and packaging strategy.	
Describe what gave rise to the problem.	
Briefly describe the problem.	
State the impact (in terms of the project objectives, such as time, cost, quality and scope).	
State how was the problem was resolved, if it was at all.	
Lesson learned: state how the problem could be avoided in the future.	

Disciplines

The project management disciplines identified may be based on the PMBOK project management areas and processes.

Procurement Route and Form of Contract

The procurement route and form of contract may be the catalyst for and the source of complexity of the problem.

Brief Description of the Problem

This description should include all relevant information, including the context. Context could include the location, project stage, topography or the adoption of novel technology. To maintain uniformity among these descriptions, it is preferable to use common labels for each of the project life cycle stages.

State the Impact

The impact should state all of the project objectives affected, such as the project schedule, capital cost, operating costs, quality and scope.

State How the Problem was Resolved

The goal of the lessons learned approach is to offer information that will be useful to managers in the future to avoid previous problems and repeat former successes where possible. Therefore, descriptions should be written so that they can be readily understood and leaving no room for misinterpretation. To achieve this result, it is recommended that descriptions are comprehensive and any acronyms are spelled out in full. A brief account of the steps adopted to solve or diminish the problem should be described.

Appendix J:
The Procurement Process

Questions to Be Answered/Decisions to Be Made During the Procurement Process

Included below is a series of questions relating to the procurement process. The decisions made on each of these subjects will determine the degree of risk that a client retains and transfers to contractors:

- What will be the process for the selection of the individual, team or party that will prepare the tender documents and evaluate the tender returns?

- Will expressions of interest be required?

- Will only pre-selected tenderers be permitted to bid?

- Will a pre-qualification (eligibility screening) process be implemented for contractors?

- How will the procurement method be chosen?

- What will be the degree of risk transfer to the contractor (to protect the client while at the same time not dissuading contractors from bidding or paying a premium for risk transfer)?

- Will a standard form of contract be selected or will the creation of a bespoke contract be necessary?

- Will amendments to the standard form of contract be introduced (if a standard form is selected)?

- What period of time will be allocated to tenderers for bidding?

- How the tender evaluation criteria will be selected?

- How much time will be allocated to the procurement process?

- What preference (if any) will be given to national contractors?

- What is the minimum number of tenders that will be acceptable?

- What are the insurance requirements?

- What weighting will be apportioned between price and technical ability?

- To what degree will the works will be subdivided (typically into packages) to obtain value for money whilst avoiding a significant number of interfaces that will be difficult to manage or will introduce the potential for claims?

- To what degree will the design be completed prior to tender?

- Will adequate time be set aside (programmed) to permit the evaluation of design information prior to tender?

- What will be the level of liquidated and ascertained damages?

- Will there be a requirement for a Performance Bond?

- Will termination or step-in rights be included?

- Which method will be used for pricing variations?

- What is the percentage of work that can be subcontracted?

- Will payment milestones be required?

- How will inflation be handled?

- How will quality be measured?

- Will stop orders be issued and, if so, on what grounds?

- What criteria will be selected for assessing suppliers and subcontractors?

Appendix K: Cybersecurity CMM

Electricity Subsector Cybersecurity Capability Maturity Model (ES-C2M2), Version 1.0, 31 May 2012

The Electricity Subsector Cybersecurity Capability Maturity Model (ES-C2M2) was developed in support of a White House initiative led by the Department of Energy (DOE), in partnership with the Department of Homeland Security (DHS) and in collaboration with asset owners and operators, the private sector and public sector experts.[1] It was developed collaboratively with an industry advisory group through a series of working sessions and was revised based on feedback from industry experts and pilot evaluations. The advisory group for the initiative included representatives from industry associations, utilities and the government. In addition, more than 40 subject-matter experts (SMEs) from industry participated in development of the model. A team of representatives from the public and private sectors developed the model in collaboration with experts from the Carnegie Mellon Software Engineering Institute (SEI).

The goal of the ES-C2M2is to support ongoing development and measurement of cybersecurity capabilities within the electricity subsector through the following four objectives:

- To strengthen cybersecurity capabilities in the electricity subsector.

- To enable utilities to effectively and consistently evaluate and benchmark cybersecurity capabilities.

---

1 The initiative used the National Infrastructure Protection Plan framework as a public-private partnership mechanism to support the development of the model. The initiative leveraged and built upon existing efforts, models and cybersecurity best practices and is aligned with strategies contained in the White House's 2010 Cyberspace Policy Review, the DOE's Roadmap to Achieve Energy Delivery Systems Cybersecurity, the Energy Sector-Specific Plan and the Industrial Control Systems Joint Working Group's Cross-Sector Roadmap for Cybersecurity of Control Systems.

- To share knowledge, best practices and relevant references within the subsector as a means to improve cybersecurity capabilities.

- To enable utilities to prioritise actions and investments in order to improve cybersecurity.

It was developed to apply to all electric utilities, regardless of ownership structure, size or function. Broad use of the model is expected to support benchmarking for the subsector's cybersecurity capabilities.

The Electricity Subsector

The electricity portion of the energy sector includes the generation, transmission, distribution and marketing of electricity. The use of electricity is ubiquitous, spanning all sectors of the US economy. The electric power subsector accounts for 40 per cent of all the energy consumed in the US. Electricity system facilities are dispersed throughout the North American continent. Although most assets are privately owned, no single organisation represents the interests of the entire subsector.

Model Architecture

The model is organized into 10 domains and 4 maturity indicator levels (MILs). Figure K.1 presents the basic structure of the model as a matrix, with domains as columns and MILs as rows.

Domains

Each of the model's 10 domains is a structured set of cybersecurity practices. Each set of practices represents the activities that an organisation can perform to establish and mature capability in the domain. For example, the risk management ("RISK") domain is a group of practices that an organisation can perform to establish and mature cybersecurity risk management capability. Each domain has a full name, such as "Risk Management," and a short name in capitals, such as "RISK". For each domain, the model provides a purpose statement, which is a high-level summary of the practices in the domain.

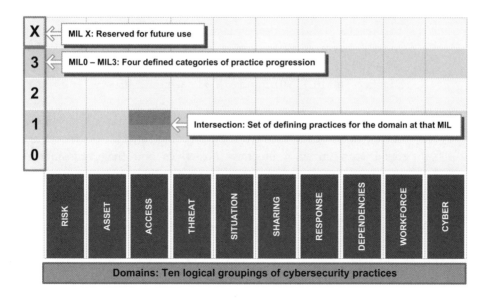

Figure K.1   Structure of the ES-C2M2

Note: Each domain is a logical grouping of cybersecurity practices. A domain's practices are organised by MIL to define the progression of capability maturity for the domain. As shown in Figure K.1, the intersection of each domain and MIL contains a set of practices that define the domain for that MIL.

Maturity Indicator Levels

The model defines four MILs (MIL0–MIL3) that apply across all the domains, and it holds a fifth MIL, MILX, in reserve for use in future versions of the model. Each of the four defined MILs is further designated by a name, for example, "MIL3: Managed". MIL0–MIL3 define the maturity progression in the model. Each MIL describes the approach and institutionalisation of the practices in a domain at that MIL. Three aspects of the MILs are important for understanding and correctly applying the model:

- The MILs apply independently to each domain. As a result, an organisation using the model may receive different MIL ratings for different domains. For example, an organisation could be functioning at MIL1 in one domain, MIL2 in another domain and MIL3 in a third domain.

- The MILs are cumulative within each domain; to earn a MIL in a given domain, an organisation must perform all of the practices in that level and its predecessor level(s). For example, an organisation must perform all of the domain practices in MIL1 and MIL2 to achieve MIL2 in the domain. Similarly, it would have to perform all practices in MIL1, MIL2 and MIL3 to achieve MIL3.

- Striving to achieve the highest MIL in all domains may not be optimal for all organisations. Practice performance and MIL achievement need to align with business objectives and the organisation's cybersecurity strategy. It is recommended that organisations familiarise themselves with the practices in the model and then determine the target levels of MIL achievement per domain. Gap analysis activities and improvement efforts should then focus on achieving these target levels.

The MILs define a dual progression of maturity: an institutionalisation progression and an approach progression, as explained in the following sections.

The 10 domains are listed below in the order in which they appear in the model. The list provides a brief description and the objectives for each domain.

Risk Management (RISK)

Establish, operate and maintain an enterprise cybersecurity risk management programme to identify, analyse and mitigate cybersecurity risk to the organisation, including its business units, subsidiaries, related interconnected infrastructure and stakeholders. RISK comprises three objectives:

1. Establish Cybersecurity Risk Management Strategy.

2. Manage Cybersecurity Risk.

3. Manage RISK Activities.

Asset, Change and Configuration Management (ASSET)

Manage the organisation's operations technology (OT) and information technology (IT) assets, including both hardware and software, commensurate with the risk to critical infrastructure and organisational objectives. ASSET comprises four objectives:

1.   Manage Asset Inventory.

2.   Manage Asset Configuration.

3.   Manage Changes to Assets.

4.   Manage ASSET Activities.

Identity and Access Management (ACCESS)

Create and manage identities for entities that may be granted logical or physical access to the organisation's assets. Control access to the organisation's assets, commensurate with the risk to critical infrastructure and organisational objectives. ACCESS comprises three objectives:

1.   Establish and Maintain Identities.

2.   Control Access.

3.   Manage ACCESS Activities.

Threat and Vulnerability Management (THREAT)

Establish and maintain plans, procedures and technologies to detect, identify, analyse, manage and respond to cybersecurity threats and vulnerabilities, commensurate with the risk to the organisation's infrastructure (e.g. critical, IT, operational) and organisational objectives. THREAT comprises three objectives:

1.   Identify and Respond to Threats.

2.   Reduce Cybersecurity Vulnerabilities.

3.   Manage THREAT Activities.

Situational Awareness (SITUATION)

Establish and maintain activities and technologies to collect, analyse, alarm, present and use power system and cybersecurity information, including status and summary information from the other model domains, to form a common operating picture (COP), commensurate with the risk to critical infrastructure and organisational objectives. SITUATION comprises four objectives:

1.   Perform Logging.

2.   Monitor the Function.

3.   Establish and Maintain a Common Operating Picture.

4.   Manage SITUATION Activities.

Information Sharing and Communications (SHARING)

Establish and maintain relationships with internal and external entities to collect and provide cybersecurity information, including threats and vulnerabilities, to reduce risks and to increase operational resilience, commensurate with the risk to critical infrastructure and organisational objectives. SHARING comprises two objectives:

1.   Share Cybersecurity Information.

2.   Manage SHARING Activities.

Event and Incident Response, Continuity of Operations (RESPONSE)

Establish and maintain plans, procedures and technologies to detect, analyse and respond to cybersecurity events and to sustain operations throughout a cybersecurity event, commensurate with the risk to critical infrastructure and organisational objectives. RESPONSE comprises five objectives:

1.   Detect Cybersecurity Events.

2.   Escalate Cybersecurity Events.

3.   Respond to Escalated Cybersecurity Events.

4.   Plan for Continuity.

5.   Manage RESPONSE Activities.

Supply Chain and External Dependencies Management (DEPENDENCIES)

Establish and maintain controls to manage the cybersecurity risks associated with services and assets that are dependent on external entities, commensurate with the risk to critical infrastructure and organisational objectives. DEPENDENCIES comprises three objectives:

1.   Identify Dependencies.

2.   Manage Dependency Risk.

3.   Manage DEPENDENCIES Activities.

Workforce Management (WORKFORCE)

Establish and maintain plans, procedures, technologies and controls to create a culture of cybersecurity, and to ensure the ongoing suitability and competence of personnel, commensurate with the risk to critical infrastructure and organisational objectives.

WORKFORCE comprises five objectives:

1.   Assign Cybersecurity Responsibilities.

2.   Control the Workforce Life Cycle.

3.   Develop Cybersecurity Workforce.

4.   Increase Cybersecurity Awareness.

5.   Manage WORKFORCE Activities.

Cybersecurity Program Management (CYBER)

Establish and maintain an enterprise cybersecurity programme that provides governance, strategic planning and sponsorship for the organisation's cybersecurity activities in a manner that aligns cybersecurity objectives with the organisation's strategic objectives and the risk to critical infrastructure. CYBER comprises five objectives:

1.   Establish Cybersecurity Programme Strategy.

2.   Sponsor Cybersecurity Programme.

3.   Establish and Maintain Cybersecurity Architecture.

4.   Perform Secure Software Development.

5.   Manage CYBER Activities.

Index

Page numbers in **bold** type refer to case studies and tables in the text.

If you have found this book useful you may be interested in other titles from Gower

Emerging Risks
A Strategic Management Guide
Edited by Catherine Antoinette Raimbault and Anne Barr
Hardback: 978-1-4094-4593-7
e-book PDF: 978-1-4094-4594-4
e-book ePUB: 978-1-4094-5938-5

Integrated Cost-Schedule Risk Analysis
David Hulett
Hardback: 978-0-566-09166-7
e-book PDF: 978-1-4094-2812-1
e-book ePUB: 978-1-4094-5910-1

Managing Project Uncertainty
David Cleden
Paperback: 978-0-566-08840-7
e-book PDF: 978-0-7546-8174-8
e-book ePUB: 978-1-4094-6050-3

Managing Risk in Projects
David Hillson
Paperback: 978-0-566-08867-4
e-book PDF: 978-0-566-09155-1
e-book ePUB: 978-1-4094-5853-1

Practical Schedule Risk Analysis
David Hulett
Hardback: 978-0-566-08790-5
e-book PDF: 978-0-7546-9196-9
e-book ePUB: 978-1-4094-5852-4

GOWER

Project Risk Analysis
Techniques for Forecasting Funding Requirements,
Costs and Timescales
Derek Salkeld
Hardback: 978-0-566-09186-5
e-book PDF: 978-1-4094-4497-8
e-book ePUB: 978-1-4094-7237-7

Strategic Project Risk Appraisal and Management
Elaine Harris
Hardback: 978-0-566-08848-3
e-book PDF: 978-0-7546-9211-9
e-book ePUB: 978-1-4094-5860-9

Tame, Messy and Wicked Risk Leadership
Edited by David Hancock
Paperback: 978-0-566-09242-8
e-book PDF: 978-1-4094-0873-4
e-book ePUB: 978-1-4094-5890-6

The Project Risk Maturity Model
Measuring and Improving Risk Management Capability
Martin Hopkinson
Hardback and CD-ROM: 978-0-566-08879-7
e-book PDF: 978-1-4094-2646-2
e-book ePUB: 978-1-4094-5895-1

Visit **www.gowerpublishing.com** and

- search the entire catalogue of Gower books in print
- order titles online at 10% discount
- take advantage of special offers
- sign up for our monthly e-mail update service
- download free sample chapters from all recent titles
- download or order our catalogue